THE
Name
OF YOUR
Game

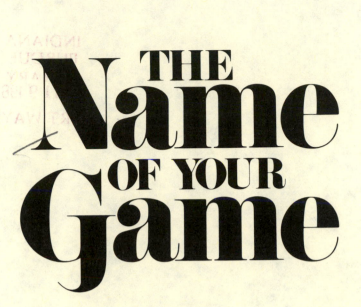

THE Name OF YOUR Game

FOUR GAME PLANS
FOR SUCCESS
AT HOME AND WORK

by

DR. STUART ATKINS

ELLIS & STEWART PUBLISHERS
Career and Life Books Division
Beverly Hills

Published by:
Ellis & Stewart Publishers
270 North Canon Drive, Suite 103
Beverly Hills, CA 90210
(213) 650-5097

Life Orientations, LIFO, Variable-Entry, Boss-Centered,
Member-Centered, One-Way, and Career and Life Management
Institute are all service and trademarks of
Stuart Atkins, Incorporated.

International Standard Book Number 0-942532-00-7
Library of Congress Catalog Number 81-71849

Printed in the United States of America

mno 8-18-83

ACKNOWLEDGMENTS

Thanks go to Drs. Freud, Erikson, Rogers, Lewin, Fromm and Maslow whose genius provided the antecedents of Life Orientations theory and Training.

I would like to thank Dr. Thomas Gordon who taught me to go beyond analysis to application, to be less concerned with the "why" and more concerned with the "how".

Thanks to Dr. James V. Clark who was responsible for my introduction into the field of group dynamics at UCLA.

I would also like to express appreciation to Dr. Allan Katcher who helped get Life Orientations Training under way and who directs it in many parts of the world.

To David Delker, there are thanks for renewal. He evoked my interest and creativity when they had waned. He has a mind that matters, and his knowledge of great ideas and thinkers is encyclopedic.

Thanks to the Union of Experimenting Colleges and Universities for the discipline and freedom to discover the deeper meaning of Life Orientations theory and Training. Particularly helpful were Drs. Ben Davis, William Harless, Gib Akin, Arthur Kovacs, Portia Shapiro and Beverly Sheiffer who ushered me into the world of advanced learning. Their standards of excellence made my learning and my book exceed my original expectations.

The LIFO Trainers across the country deserve special thanks for helping shape and hone my thinking during 10 years of Life Orientations Seminars for Professionals.

Pamela C. Raffetto, my publications manager, must know my daily appreciation of her value. Her gentle criticism, literary taste and her intelligence combine to guide my judgment about what appropriately communicates.

Thanks to Dr. Arthur Kovacs who made many useful recommendations about the content and structure of the book. Over the years, he has provided warmth and wisdom which has guided my development as a person and as a professional.

CONTENTS

INTRODUCTION

For years, we have been told about our weaknesses, about what is wrong with us. As an antidote to this negative approach, this book will focus on our strengths—what is right about us. It will accentuate the positive and the possible.

There will be no recommendations to change ourselves. Rather, I will present strategies to show how we can get the most from our strengths, and from the strengths of the key people in our lives. I will demonstrate how to manage our strengths and forget about our weaknesses.

The book will also show how we are oriented to life. Oriented means the direction we take through it, our game plan for life. This plan generates our strengths, and determines how we treat people and what is really important to us.

There are four such game plans. I have called them Supporting-Giving, Controlling-Taking, Conserving-Holding and Adapting-Dealing. These four orientations are the basis of our choices and actions.

By knowing our game plan and the game plan of key people in our lives, we can improve our strengths, and theirs as well. With the knowledge of our game plans, we can influence and communicate with others faster, more clearly, and with greater impact.

Finally, by knowing which game plan we prefer *least,* we will have answers to why we are vulnerable to making major mistakes, and vulnerable to overlooking important opportunities in our lives.

The Name of Your Game reflects the influence of past and contemporary masters in human behavior. One of these is psychologist Carl Rogers and his client-centered counseling. This is reflected in the fact that the language and the ideas in the book are constructed to be as non-judgmental as possible, and to communicate in ways that show "unconditional positive regard" for people. This means putting aside thoughts of right or wrong, good or bad, considering only what will facilitate us, knowing that facilitation is fostered in the absence of critical analysis and in the presence of self-acceptance.

The book also follows principles of psychologist Abraham Maslow, with his emphasis on developing and helping "healthy" people grow stronger—in his terms, actualizing them to tap their fuller potential. There is no ideal model of a person to become, no model anything, and no norms or standards to live up to. There is only the wish for people to liberate what is individually within themselves, their potential.

The discoveries of Life Orientations® Training, called LIFO® Training for short, upon which this book is based, started in the United States in 1968. It was first applied in such diverse organizations as General Foods, U.S. Steel, The American Cancer Society, State of California, Global Marine, and Mattel Toys.

Since that time, industry, hospitals, schools, government, churches and universities have put Life Orientations Training into practice to help people be more productive and more satisfied. Teachers, students, foremen, psychologists, doctors, nurses, policemen, firemen, executives, parents, children, husbands, and wives have had Life Orientations Training. As a result of the theory and training, they acquired new strategies to help them succeed at home and at work.

Over 5,000 organizations and over one million men, women and children throughout the world have had their lives influenced by Life Orientations Training and the new strength-building success strategies it recommends. I hope that you are influenced by it, too, and that this book makes a difference in your life.

Stuart Atkins, Ph.D.
Beverly Hills, California
1982

1

THE NAME
OF MY GAME

A PRACTICAL WAY
TO SOLVE PEOPLE PROBLEMS

It was the beginning of 1967. I thought that I was making the world turn my way, and my game plan was to help make the world a more human place in which to live and work.

I had been heavily involved with the National Training Laboratories out of Washington, D.C. for three years as a group leader in human relations training. At the same time, I was deeply engaged in my own organizational consulting practice throughout the United States, helping with people-problems in industry, government, hospitals, universities, and schools.

I was conducting a one-day workshop in New York, a three-day workshop in Boston, a five-day program in Texas, a two-day conference in Northern California. The participants were people from different organizations and from different professions—from engineers to church executives, from sales people to school teachers, from psychologists to production managers.

Wearily I said to a colleague, "I have to stop traveling. I've got to get better organized and do work in my own back yard, here in Southern California."

He shook his head in disbelief, and said not too kindly, "Atkins, the trouble with you is you're a chipmunk chaser."

Being raised in the city and not the country, I said, "I don't know what you're talking about. I don't know what a chipmunk does."

He smiled wryly, "Well, a chipmunk preparing for the winter sees a nut, goes over and grabs it, and starts out to hide it in a tree. But on his way, he sees another nut. He drops the first one, grabs the second, and heads out for the tree again. He drops what he has and runs to grab another, then another, all the way to the tree. When he finally reaches the tree with one nut, he is exhausted. If he had been more systematic and taken one nut at a time, he would have a large winter's supply with less effort.

"You're just like that chipmunk. You're chasing after all the nuts that you can, and you're holding on to very few. You need to get organized," he said. "You need to build on what you have."

He hit home. But I was still confused. That was not my game plan. I followed the belief that opportunity knocks once, and you have to seize the opportunity. You had better move quickly, and not hold on too long to the old. You had to move on to something new and novel, something challenging. Group work was a challenge for me at that time. I had a sense of mission. I was teaching people how to feel. How to expand their lives. To be self-actualized. That was a big term for us. And all they had to do was *feel*, express those feelings, say it like it is, be open and honest, and be confrontational.

Somehow, by a magical process, the air would be cleared, and relationships would improve. Disclosure and feedback were big with us, too. Say it like you feel it, tell it like you see it—this could only make one's life better. With this mission, a cure for personal and organizational ills, there was no time to waste.

Somehow I thought, despite my friend's admonition about being a chipmunk, that I was destined to be a chipmunk—forever. There was no way I could visualize myself taking things a step at a time; being that orderly, that methodical. I didn't have the patience for it, let alone believe in the value of it.

From my point of view, it would only slow me down. There was too much to do, too many places to go, too many groups to help. The prospect of working with a new group excited me. Next week I would be working with doctors. I'd never worked with them before. What would I encounter? Would they be the same or different from school teachers, university professors, engineers? Would they respond to group dynamics? Could I have an impact on their lives? Could I teach them more about themselves and how to get along? That was the challenge. That was the satisfaction.

Slow down? Restrict my activities? Think more, organize better? It didn't seem worth it. Life for me was beautiful when I had something new, novel and challenging. I liked the whirlwind. (I didn't realize that I was struggling between two orientations to life, two game plans, that I would come to call Controlling-Taking and Conserving-Holding.)

Tell me something couldn't be done, tell me that the group next week would probably resist Human Relations training, and I would be exhilarated by the challenge and the chance to prove my mastery. That was the name of my game.

The early 1960's was a golden time for me, yet a time of overcommitment and weariness. It was a time when expressing feelings was not permissible. It was a time when social politeness ruled our human encounters, our exchanges as people. It was a time when men could not express affection and tenderness. We seldom said it like it was. If we did, it was with rage, or fury, or bitterness, from being bottled up so long.

So there we were, applied behavioral scientists, and NTL trainers with our group methods, being forerunners of EST, Assertiveness Training, Marriage Encounters, Fighting Fair, Intimacy Training. We were norm fighters, trying to change the standards of society, making it OK to feel and to express anything and everything in the service of maturing as people and getting along.

We were trying to combat being closed-mouthed with thoughts and feelings, trying to wipe out the practice of second guessing each other. We were fighting for people—including ourselves—who had lived and worked together for years and who still did not know each other. We did not know each other because of our fear of sharing our inner thoughts and feelings.

Some colleagues and I believed that we could teach organizations to be like families. Work could be a place where people could let their hair down, where they still could be people, even though they had a role to perform.

My colleagues and I believed that by the expression of feelings and the disclosure of withheld information, people could build bridges between their roles, cross over and relate to each other as people while doing a job. We dreamt of the role and the person as being one. Yes, and we had words and concepts for it: being congruent, being authentic. We gave thanks to Drs. Carl Rogers, Jim Bugental, and Sidney Jourard, whose imagination and intelligence gave us the concepts.

But eventually, people in organizations were beginning to tell us, "You can't do this. This is not our family. This is where we work. People have power over us. We can get fired, be denied promotions. It's too much to risk, too dangerous to be authentic and open where you work. You don't dare tell people what you think, or express your feelings.

"If you want to teach us more about ourselves, how to get along, do it in a way that doesn't put us at such risk. Give us something that is more structured, where we don't have to take such chances hurting each other's feelings and putting our jobs in jeopardy."

It was from such admonitions that Life Orientations Training—LIFO® Training for short—was born.

From February until December of 1967, the rudiments of Life Orientations theory were developed, along with the Life Orientations Survey. The Survey helped people classify their orientations to life, their basic game plan, and their strengths as people.

By early 1968, the Life Orientations survey received its maiden presentations by me and my partner, Dr. Allan Katcher, at such diverse organizations as the American Cancer Society, Global Marine, Inc., and Mattel; then at General Foods, U.S. Steel, State of California, Department of Employment, and in my classes in Human Factors in Management at UCLA.

People were fascinated with their survey results. They enjoyed the language of the survey. They enjoyed being able to identify the name of their game—Supporting-Giving, Controlling-Taking, Conserving-Holding, and Adapting-Dealing.

These were simple labels for proven ways of being successful. Here are capsule definitions for each.

SUPPORTING-GIVING: Good comes from hard work and the pursuit of excellence. Thoughtful, trusting, idealistic, loyal. Tries to do the very best; sets high standard for self, and others.

CONTROLLING-TAKING: Good comes from seizing opportunity, being competent. Bottomline, results-oriented. A go-getter. Tends to act quickly, makes things happen. Self-confident, persuasive, competitive.

CONSERVING-HOLDING: Good comes from making the most of what you have and using your head. Methodical, logical, precise, tenacious. Before acting, tries to analyze every angle; looks always for the fail-safe way to do a job. Practical, reserved.

ADAPTING-DEALING: Good comes from pleasing others, filling their needs. Gets to know people. Frequently characterized as flexible, enthusiastic, tactful, inspiring, charming. Tries to get along, has empathy.

Suddenly, with this common language, people had new ways to describe themselves; they could compare how they were similar or different. This hunger to compare amazed me—people's eagerness to see how they stack up against each other.

They also wanted to know what was the "best" orientation, the best game plan. What should they be? What should they do? They asked for norms, and wanted to measure themselves against a standard.

It was very difficult for them to accept the fact that in the Life Orientations model there was no one best way, no norm. Actually, it was self-normative. We compared people against themselves, their own wishes, their own choices, their own strengths, how well they executed their life plan. We wanted to profile their uniqueness—what was the best *of* them, what was the best *for* them.

After people's initial curiosity was satisfied, other questions began to arise. So what? What can we *do* with this information?

How does it affect our relationships with other people?

What does it mean if my game plan is Controlling-Taking and my boss's plan is Conserving-Holding?

Why is there no one best orientation?—no one best game plan?

What is the difference to me if I prefer Supporting-Giving and don't use Controlling-Taking?

Why can't I get more people to look at things from my orientation?—to follow my game plan?

As I answered these questions, I began to build Life Orientations Training, with its success strategies for making the most of the game plans. I called the strategies Confirming, Capitalizing, Moderating, Supplementing, Extending and Bridging.

Without realizing it, I was becoming more structured, more systematic, and I was using more logic. I was also becoming less like a chipmunk running around collecting nuts unsystematically for the winter. I was using more of the Conserving-Holding game plan, and I was developing the Extending strategy.

That's what this book is all about: Expanding our game plan to see new opportunities and solve old problems; learn what to do when our game plan conflicts with the plans of the key people in our lives—bosses, parents, children, teachers and intimate partners—at home and at work.

Success and failure revolve around our use and misuse of our game plan. By better understanding the name of our game, and helping others to do the same, we can stack the cards in our favor.

Here are the success strategies for the best use of our game plan:

1. CONFIRMING
Know our game plan, our strengths and uniqueness.

2. CAPITALIZING
Seek situations which bring out our best strengths and allow us to follow our game plan.

3. MODERATING
Avoid overusing favorite game plans and strengths to the point of excess.

16

4. *SUPPLEMENTING*
   Get help from people with different game plans and strengths.

5. *EXTENDING*
   Learn to use some of the strengths from different game plans for ourselves.

6. *BRIDGING*
   Improve communications with people who have different game plans and strengths.

2

TURNING WEAKNESSES INTO STRENGTHS

DISCOVERIES OF
LIFE ORIENTATIONS® TRAINING

I have been surprised by how few people are aware of their strengths and excesses. The idea has been around since the 5th Century, B.C. Yet, excess is the number one complaint people level against us at work and at home.

Whether I am working with a front-line foreman or a company president, a minister or a salesperson, psychologist, engineer, professor, doctor or lawyer, they all have their excesses.

At home or at work, the complaints about us, or our complaints about other people, can be distilled down to four general excesses.

Trying too hard and giving too much
  (Supporting-Giving).

Moving too fast and coming on too strong
  (Controlling-Taking).

Moving too slow, and holding on too long
  (Conserving-Holding).

Staying too loose and going along too far
  (Adapting-Dealing).

These excesses are nothing more than the strengths of our game plan pushed to the point of exaggeration, to the point of doing too much of a good thing, from overplaying our game. Excess and strengths are linked together in one package. We don't have one without the other.

Take the first general excess—trying too hard and giving too much. That excess comes from the Supporting-Giving game plan, with its strengths of trying to do our best and trying to do what is right and fair for others.

But this very strength, when overused, becomes a striving for perfection that can ultimately lead us to neglect our own well being because we are trying to accomplish the impossible.

Let me illustrate. At work, Frank's boss says about him, "He's really great at bringing people along for promotions. He backs them up. He shows confidence in them, trusts them. And he expects the best from them—and he gets it. They react by being involved, making an extra effort. He lets go of the reins, and they take on more responsibility. His group admires and respects him.

"On the other hand, he can be very critical—about management and his people. He expects a lot. He shoots for the moon. What unbelievable standards! But he always worries whether he's doing what's right and fair by everybody, and they take advantage of him. He tries so hard to help everybody that he takes on more than he should, and sometimes doesn't deliver on his promises because he's taken on more than he can handle."

The second excess—moving too fast and coming on too strong—comes from the game plan I call Controlling-Taking, with its strength of initiating and taking charge. But it can lead to being impulsive and domineering.

John, a senior in high school, describes his mother. "Mom's a real powerhouse. She really stands up for what she wants. She has so much energy, she's into everything. She's a real go-getter. She's always trying things she's never tried before. Tell her she can't do something and she'll find a way to do it. When we have a family discussion, and we can't make up our minds, she'll make the decision for us.

"But sometimes, I wish she'd think before she leaps. Like when we sold our house before we bought another one. And when we talk, she'll be the first one to tell her ideas and opinions. She'll argue a point until you have to give in just to get her off your back. Too many times she doesn't give us a chance to show what we know, what we can do. It doesn't look like she trusts us."

The third excess—moving too slow and holding on too long—comes from the Conserving-Holding game plan. These excesses are attached to the strengths of reasoning things out, moving a step at a time, and staying with things until the facts show there is something better. But thinking precisely and staying with what we have until the facts prove otherwise can cause analysis-paralysis and keep us stuck on dead center.

Mrs. Harris talks about her husband. "When you've got a thorny problem, one that requires you to understand all sides of it, I like to go to Joe. He really gets into things, takes it apart and shows you what's really going on, things you'd never think of. When he wants you to do something, he gives you the reasons. He's calm, cool, and collected. It gives me the feeling I'm on solid ground. And with our tight budget, he knows how to make the most out of what we've got.

"Sometimes, though, I wish he'd get more excited about things, just give an answer off the top of his head. By the time you get a decision from Joe, the opportunity may be gone, or you've lost interest. Like planning our vacation, he analyzes things to death, getting entangled in all the possibilities and places. It confuses me. And when he wants his way, he piles on the facts until they weigh you down, or you see the light. Just once in a while, I'd like to see him bust loose, let go, have more fun."

The fourth excess—staying too loose and going along too far—comes from Adapting-Dealing with its strengths of being open to all points of view, trying it their way, and keeping disagreement smoothed over with a light touch.

But the readiness to be flexible, to go along with others, can be pushed to an excess. It can divert us from our own goals, and can make us unfocused and inconsistent. Smoothing things over with a light touch can be exaggerated until we placate others and prevent serious problems from getting the airing they need.

Phil talks about his sweetheart. "Sally is very popular. Everybody likes her. She gets along well with my family, my friends. When I have an argument with my parents, Sally is the peacemaker. When I get too heavy about things, she brings me out of it with her light touch. She makes sure we have fun. She knows exactly what mood I'm in. Another thing I like, she's quick to get my message. I always get the feeling she understands me. Before she tries to get her way, she'll go along with my ideas first.

"But sometimes, she's so agreeable I don't know where she's coming from. I'm not saying she'll 'yes' you all the time, but I wish she would show her own conviction, stand firm. I don't like it when she appeases me. And there are times when she jumps to the rescue too soon, won't let people clear the air with a good fight. She jokes too much and I can't get her to talk seriously about some of our problems."

The weaknesses which irritate, annoy, or even exasperate us about people are simply an exaggeration, an excess, of the very same strengths we like and admire in them.

To control our excesses, we first must be aware that they are attached to strengths. It is not necessary to throw away our strengths—only the excess. We need to avoid doing too much of a good thing. If we can, we save time and energy. Strengths don't have to boomerang and come back to us by rubbing people the wrong way and defeating our purpose.

During my 25 years as an organizational consultant, I have discovered a second roadblock to our success and satisfaction. We do not know what we do not know!

That's more than a play on words. What I mean is that we all have *blind spots* which prevent us from seeing certain obvious facts around us, which prevent us from capitalizing on our strengths. We are not aware of valuable information available to us for planning, solving problems, and for making crucial decisions about our lives.

When we make mistakes, get into trouble, or don't accomplish our goals, we frequently say, "I can't figure it out. What went wrong? What did I miss?" Someone else in the situation says, "Have you ever thought of this?" "This" turns out to be the solution. They had an entirely different way of looking at it.

Then we say, "Now why did I overlook it? Why didn't I think of that?"

The answer is, we seldom, if ever, think of that! We seldom look at things that way. It's not one of our usual strengths. It's not in our game plan. It's our blind spot, a missing perspective. It's not the name of our game.

If we are to avoid major mistakes and see new opportunities, we need to see the world from the four major orientations to life, the four game plans.

With 95% of us, at least one game plan is missing. We do not think that way often, and we seldom use those strengths. Either we simply neglect that game plan because we don't value it, or we have not been exposed to it, or we are irritated or angered by it.

But all four game plans, all four sets of strengths, are needed to give us *total perspective and added control* over our life, with its problems and people. The additional information and strength from this *total* view can aid our judgment in the execution of our work and our wishes.

The third discovery for me is the fallacy of the "Golden Rule." It doesn't work in communications with each other. We can't treat people the way *we* want to be treated. Actually, there are four basic ways people want to be treated. They want us to approach them emphasizing *their* orientations, their game plan of Supporting-Giving, Controlling-Taking, Conserving-Holding, or Adapting-Dealing. We may favor Supporting-Giving, but they may respond to approaches favoring Adapting-Dealing.

Depending on what game plan we emphasize, we assume our way is the general way and certainly the best way. So we "do unto others the way we want them to do unto us." But they want to be done unto the way *they* prefer—which may be our *least* preferred way!

Then the trouble starts. It's my way versus your way. My strengths versus your strengths. Then we say, "Be reasonable, do it my way!" For example, you may say, "We've got to go faster to seize the opportunity." I may counter, "We need more time to think it through better, or we'll blow the chance anyway."

I may say, "We have to get them to like it." And you may reply, "We know what's best for them, whether they like it or not."

You may declare, "The facts speak for themselves." And I may plead, "If we don't work to get the facts accepted, nobody will do anything about them."

Supporting-Giving, Controlling-Taking, Conserving-

Holding, and Adapting-Dealing are constantly vying for position as we work and live together. Which one will go first? Which game plan will lead the way? Which will fall by the wayside as we dispute our differences?

My-way-or-your-way is the most tension-producing, dissatisfying, time-wasting, energy-draining, relationship-breaking activity known to man, woman, or child.

Without a doubt, we need each other's strengths, each other's differences. But there is no need to lose our uniqueness or give up our game plan. In the Life Orientations model, we can use each other's differences without changing ourselves, without denying who we are or what we stand for.

The Life Orientations model helps us live with our differences and make more sense to each other. It reduces misunderstandings and conflict. It can replace frustration and excess with productivity and satisfaction.

But before you read more about the Life Orientations Viewpoint, I would like you to examine the questions listed below. They will help you pinpoint your priorities, what's most important for you to get out of this book.

12 LIFE PRIORITY QUESTIONS

√ *CHECK FOUR QUESTIONS YOU CONSIDER TOP PRIORITY*

__ 1. What is my game plan?

__ 2. What are my strengths as a person?

__ 3. What is the best way to get me to use my strengths?

__ 4. What kinds of situations stimulate me and will bring out the best in me?

__ 5. What is the best way for others to communicate with me to manage my strengths?

__ 6. What new approaches to people and problems do I need to try?

— 7. What kinds of pressures and conditions create stress for me?

— 8. How do I exaggerate my strengths and become excessive, creating self-defeating action?

— 9. How can I or others curb my excesses?

— 10. What new relationship strategies will assist me in influencing key people in my life?

— 11. What kinds of people work well with me?

— 12. What kinds of people do I find it hard to work with?

You might want to discuss your choices with someone close to you. You might even have them check the questions that are top priority for *them.* Then you could compare your choices and discuss why you chose them. You will discover some useful information about yourselves and each other.

3

THE NAME
OF YOUR GAME

FOUR GAME PLANS
TO GUIDE YOUR LIFE

Life starts with us in the center of things.

It is as if we are born into the center of a room with four walls. There is a window on each wall looking out to the world.

Because of our life experiences, and what has worked for us, we look at the world through one or two windows of our choice. We may learn to look through the window in front of us and to the right of us. Someone else may look at the world from the windows to our left and behind us.

When we try to describe the world to each other, it appears as if we are talking about two different worlds. It's really the same world out there, but we're only describing our familiar perspective, our preferred orientation, the game plan that has been reinforced through trial and error, success and failure.

Difficulty between us can start when we try to work or live together, if your views of the world come from opposite windows. Trouble happens when my way of looking at the world is from the window in front of me, and your way of looking at the world is from the window behind me. I may have occasionally looked out that window, but it's been infrequent, and I don't remember how things are from there.

I choose to remember my comforting viewpoint, my own convenient perspective.

But that is not enough. We need *total* perspective. No person's judgment is any better than the completeness and accuracy of their information. And if we get information from only one or two windows, we are missing important knowledge. Then we do not have everything available to bring to a problem or a decision affecting our lives and each other.

We need people who are different from us. They have a different perspective and different strengths. We need them by having them physically present, or by learning to ask the unique questions they would ask if they were with us, the questions that come from their orientation to life.

What this book does is broaden our awareness of the *total* world outside our room, the total perspective and the total power available to us through different game plans. We can go beyond our present state of working and loving from the limited information we get from our select view of the world.

In 1566, Andrea Palladio, an Italian architect, designed and built a structure called La Rotonda near Vicenza, Italy. (Figure 1, page 27). He solved the problem of total perspective with a 360° view. His structure, La Rotonda, was built on a hill overlooking a valley. He accomplished total perspective by backing up four classical Greek temples to each other and unifying them with a dome.

Inside, the structure is a large, high circular hall, a rotunda. On the outside, there are four *fronts,* four porticos with their columns and steps facing in four different directions. From the four porticos, the four fronts, there is a total and commanding view of the valley below. La Rotonda is oriented north, south, east and west!

As people, however, our orientation is not in every direction. How we are oriented to life directs us down the valley from our Rotonda along a certain path with a plan for life. We need first to capitalize on the strengths and uniqueness of our life path and plan. And we need to better understand others who may have chosen a path down to the other side of the valley.

In short, by understanding all four plans, we can live better, work better, and love better when we are confronted with unfamiliar or displeasing ways of going through the world.

Figure 1—La Rotonda

As I have stated earlier, there are four orientations. I call them *Supporting-Giving, Controlling-Taking, Conserving-Holding,* and *Adapting-Dealing.* It is important to understand each orientation. They are the center of things, and they contain the basic game plan upon which we operate. If we are to better understand how these plans interplay within ourselves, and between us and other people, we need to highlight them with their goals and their strengths.

The tables that follow show the sequence of my Life Orientations viewpoint—orientation, game plan, goals, strengths.

Can You Identify Your Most Preferred and Least Preferred Orientations?

27

THE FOUR ORIENTATIONS TO LIFE
Which are your most and least preferred?

SUPPORTING-GIVING ORIENTATION

GAME PLAN
If I prove my worth by working hard and seeking excellence, the good things of life will come to me.

GOALS
Do What is Right, Be Helpful

STRENGTHS
Principled • Cooperative • Dedicated • Loyal

CONTROLLING-TAKING ORIENTATION

GAME PLAN
If I get results by being competent and seizing opportunity, the good things in life will be there for the taking.

GOALS
Be in Charge, Get Results

STRENGTHS
Persistent • Initiating • Urgent • Directing

CONSERVING-HOLDING ORIENTATION

GAME PLAN
If I think before I act and make the most of what I've got, I can build up my supply of the good things in life.

GOALS
Be Reasonable, Make Sure

STRENGTHS
Systematic • Analytical • Maintaining • Tenacious

ADAPTING-DEALING ORIENTATION

GAME PLAN
If I please other people and fill their needs first, then I can get the good things in life that I've wanted all along.

GOALS
Know People, Get Along

STRENGTHS
Tactful • Flexible • Aware • Sociable

THE LIFE ORIENTATIONS SEQUENCE OF HUMAN ACTION

The way we are oriented leads to a game plan, then to personal goals, which in turn lead to our strengths.

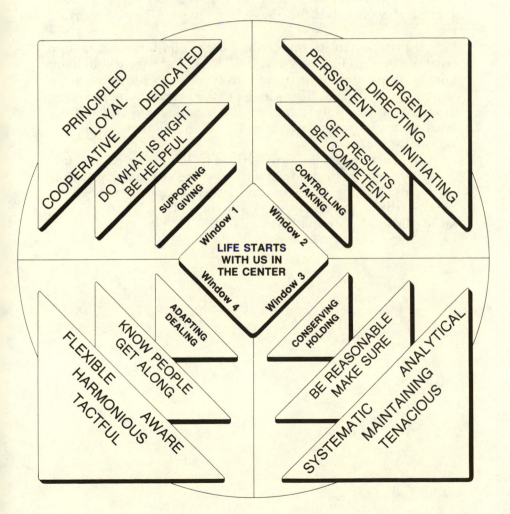

29

While one's path through life is controlled by genetics and chance, making up one's mind and choosing what to do and where to go shapes one's destiny. Underlying our choices and actions are the four orientations to life, the game plans— *Supporting-Giving, Controlling-Taking, Conserving-Holding,* and *Adapting-Dealing.* These four influence what we decide, what we expect, what we give and get throughout our lives.

They pervade everything we do. We may not put these plans into words, but they have been there. They are part of us.

It is important to understand each orientation no matter what our *own* preferences may be. This knowledge will help us communicate more effectively with the key people in our lives who may be different. Knowledge of the orientations and their strengths will help us to better understand what motivates us, what makes us experience stress, and enable us to capitalize on our strengths.

For each of us, the orientations to life are at our center. If we are to better understand how these interplay within ourselves, and between us and other people, we need to review them carefully and see how they lead to our strengths—and potential excess.

4

STRENGTHS
OF OUR GAME

OUR CLAIM TO FAME

In the previous chapter, each orientation, its game plan, goals
and its strengths were highlighted to give you an overview.
What follows is a more in-depth examination of the four
orientations—*Supporting-Giving, Controlling-Taking, Conserving-
Holding,* and *Adapting-Dealing.*

In these explanations, there is a description of what is
"right" about each of them. No judgment is intended. But
notice, as you read them, how your own preferences will color
the credibility and acceptance of them.

THE SUPPORTING-GIVING ORIENTATION
AND ITS STRENGTHS

First, consider Supporting-Giving. Its basic game plan
revolves around the key theme of *proving one's worth.* Someone
who lives by the Supporting-Giving orientation summarizes
their philosophy by saying, "I have to prove my worth because
nothing is coming to me. I have to earn it.

"I can prove my worth by being a principled
person—someone who seeks excellence, does the right thing,
and does the very best possible. Another way I can prove my
worth is by being a responsive and cooperative person. I'm
there when you need me.

"Then, if I've been a good person—followed my principles, done what's right and proper for myself and others—people will recognize my worth. They'll appreciate my good works, and the good things of life will come to me. I will be rewarded in kind, without ever having to ask."

Those who follow the Supporting-Giving orientation communicate some profound principles. First of all, they say that they have to prove their worth; they don't come on this earth already acceptable. Their existence is not enough. Their worth must be proven—continuously. Often when they do, it is done quietly, modestly. Good works are anonymous when possible. The saying goes, "Virtue is its own reward."

People often ask me, "Well, isn't this the Protestant work ethic?" I reply, of course, "Yes." However, psychoanalysts would say that, more fundamentally, the work ethic had come from a character orientation. They would probably go further and say that the Protestant work ethic grew up as a natural consequence from the people who experienced certain training in their early childhood development. But we are not focusing on origins. We are looking at ourselves operating today in the here and now.

A close friend of mine described his Supporting-Giving way. He said, "If you want to succeed in life, then cast your bread upon the waters, and it will come back to you a clubhouse sandwich."

The Avis Rent-A-Car advertising campaign says, "We're #2. We try harder." Definitely a Supporting-Giving statement, appealing most strongly to people with this orientation.

"If it's worth doing at all, it's worth doing well" is a Supporting-Giving saying, too. Another is, "If you can't do it right, don't do it at all." Another is John F. Kennedy's "Ask not what your country can do for you, but what you can do for your country."

In working with people, I can always tell if their *least* preferred orientation is Supporting-Giving. What will happen is this. I give the description of Supporting-Giving game plan. They look quizzical, shake their heads. Then a question follows: "How can a person be so naive, expect things to come to them—just if they're a good person doing their very best? Who cares how much good is in a project or idea; does it work, does it get results—that's what counts! And how can you trust people that much? You'll just get hurt, disappointed. That won't work. The world doesn't go that way—unless you're a saint!"

These doubters of the Supporting-Giving way focus on the *excess,* the extreme of trusting others, when it becomes gullibility; the extreme of pursuing excellence, when it becomes unusable perfection.

Nevertheless, the Supporting-Giving game plan works—for many people. It gets them what they want. And they get along, the way *they* want to get along. They feel successful and *are* successful, in *every* walk of life, in every occupation, and every level of our society.

Below is a summary of some of the Supporting-Giving strengths.
- Keeping an eye on quality rather than quantity.
- Keeping relevant goals in focus.
- Getting cooperation from others.
- Being responsive to the needs of others.
- Doing what is right and fair and just.
- Seeing a vision of a better future.

The name of the game is *excellence.* Excellence comes through leading an exemplary life, being principled and helpful, trying hard and doing good.

THE CONTROLLING-TAKING ORIENTATION AND ITS STRENGTHS

Controlling-Taking is certainly a contrast. People who follow this plan place major emphasis on *doing.* Not believing. They say, "I care less about what you believe and more about what you do. If you show what you can do, demonstrate competency, and get results, then you can make it in this world. It's the bottom line that counts."

They'll tell you exactly what they expect. You'll more frequently know where they stand and what they want. They say, "You have to be aware of opportunities, and seize them. You can't wait for things to come to you. The good things in life are there for the taking.

"But no matter what you do, no matter what you accomplish, you still can't wait for the rewards to come to you.

You must reach out, pull them in, take them. Don't be naive, if you don't reach out, you're going to be passed up."

Now, people who *least* prefer Controlling-Taking often say to me, "Isn't someone who has that philosophy an opportunist?", to which I reply, "No, he or she is a *person* who seeks opportunity."

When you say a person *is* an opportunist, you're putting them in a box marked "opportunist." It implies, watch out for them everywhere and on all occasions. I'd rather we say they are acting in an opportunistic way. Using the word "acting" conveys fluid behavior, not fixed for all time and all situations.

Nevertheless, even when we say they are acting in an opportunistic way, we're beginning to describe the *excess* of Controlling-Taking. For example, a strength of Controlling-Taking is being enterprising. A person can be acting in a very enterprising way, searching for opportunities, being clever and making things happen. The excess, or exaggeration, is acting opportunistically, seizing the opportunity at all costs—or at somebody else's expense.

People who do not have a high preference for Controlling-Taking will often say, "This sounds like the businessperson, the entrepreneur, somebody who gets out there and hustles and bustles around the country, going from place to place, project to project. They act out the beer commercial, 'You only go around once, so you've got to grab all the gusto you can'." But Controlling-Taking is not the sole province of business people, and people who are active and successful in business may prefer any of the four orientations.

Those who prefer Controlling-Taking feel that "Opportunity knocks but once," and that "God helps those who help themselves." They follow the sayings "Time waits for no man," and "Time is of the essence." Other characteristic sayings are "Actions speak louder than words," and "Nothing ventured, nothing gained."

Exploring Controlling-Taking further, imagine people playing cards. Someone with Controlling-Taking wins the hand. The chips are in the center of the table. This person thinks, "I've got to reach out and pull them in. Nobody's going to push them to me. I have to take the reward."

It would be quite different with someone who favors Supporting-Giving. In this case, the person has won the hand, and played it superbly, with excellence. People comment on the clever way in which the hand was played. The chips are piled in the center of the table. Some pleasant banter takes place and before you know it, someone takes the pile of chips and pushes it in the direction of our winner. He or she smiles modestly, but is inwardly pleased at excelling and playing the very best hand possible.

But with Controlling-Taking, as soon as the desired results are realized, and the sooner the better, there is no waiting for the reward. It's theirs, and it's there for the taking—now.

Below is a summary of some of the Controlling-Taking strengths.
- Creating a sense of urgency to get things started or finished.
- Organizing others and taking charge of uncertain situations.
- Sensing opportunities and what's required to seize them.
- Being willing to confront and bargain hard for a fair share.
- Staying with a difficult and challenging situation.

The name of the game is Action. There is an urgency. And when there's a vacuum and opportunity, it's time to move in for fear the opportunity will pass by, never to come again.

THE CONSERVING-HOLDING ORIENTATION AND ITS STRENGTHS

In Conserving-Holding, the game plan centers around *reason*. If we want to succeed, we've got to *think* before we act. God gave us a brain, we had better use it.

We have to look around us, take into account what's already there and build on it. We must make the most of what we've got. If we do, we can build up a supply of the good things in life. And if we store the things we need, they'll be there when we want them.

With Conserving-Holding, getting results is important but accuracy and completeness are more so. Being right in the sense of this accuracy and correctness is essential. It is different from being "right and proper," doing the "right" thing, the principled thing, as in the Supporting-Giving orientation.

Another emphasis with Conserving-Holding is on certainty and logic. Everything needs to *fit,* sensibly. When things make sense, there is a certainty. Then we have security because things are predictable. To gain predictability, we must have accuracy and completeness. We must examine everything in depth, look for alternatives and predict consequences.

A key here is that we want no surprises. We don't want to be blind-sided. And while most of us don't enjoy too much uncertainty, the person who follows the Conserving-Holding way has a lower threshold for surprises. A small error, an omission, more quickly surprises. Orderliness brings stability and predictability, "A place for everything and everything in its place."

Rushing around doesn't make sense. "Activity doesn't mean productivity," they say. "Well thought out action can save time and money."

To succeed, we need to take things a step at a time. This avoids the possibility of "falling off the deep end." We need to go slow and be sure. And finally, with Conserving-Holding, we don't have to reach out and grab things, nor do we have to wait until our worth is recognized. And we don't have to look over the fence into everybody else's back yard looking for something that's better. We cultivate our own garden.

Voltaire's character Candide traveled all over the world searching for something better, having adventures and misadventures. After years of travel with his Controlling-Taking game plan, looking for something new and novel, he comes home and changes his plan: "Cultivate your own garden," he says. He now prefers Conserving-Holding. Candide's realization is that everything he needs is right where he started from. He concludes that you don't have to go far from home to find the good life. You can discover all manner of riches in your own back yard.

With Conserving-Holding, "Change for change's sake" has no meaning. The change has to be for practical reasons, and sound evidence for the change must be presented.

By administering the Life Orientations Survey to the key executives in one organization, I discovered that all of them had Conserving-Holding as their most preferred game plan.

I couldn't believe how level-headed they appeared in meetings. There was such calm and reserve, such rationality. Sweet reason prevailed.

They would calmly discuss sensitive issues about personalities, designing new products, and profitability. Such factual step-by-step explanations and explorations!

But because of the predominance of only this one style, I found myself asking, "Where's the enthusiasm? Where's the gung-ho spirit to rally 'round the flag and get things moving?" But everything seemed to be handled quite well, a step at a time. They made decisions only after careful exploration and deliberation.

With Conserving-Holding, the motto is, "Think now, act later," because "You better look before you leap."

Below is a summary of some of the Conserving-Holding strengths.
- Utilizing what you've got before trying something new.
- Taking things a step at a time to cover all bases.
- Thinking before acting, and checking facts.
- Weighing the pros and cons, and seeing trade-offs in situations.
- Keeping a cool head in the midst of crisis.

The name of the game is Reason. Using our head to make the most of what we've got keeps us going. Be sure to tie the old to the new, and don't forget the "tried and true."

THE ADAPTING-DEALING ORIENTATION AND ITS STRENGTHS

People oriented to Adapting-Dealing describe their game plan this way. "If you want to succeed in the world, then you have to find out what people think and feel, help them get what they want. After you do, then you can ask for the things that you've wanted all along.

"To please people, to win them over, they must come first. To accomplish this, you have to be finely tuned to people's feelings and listen to what they say and what they don't say."

With this information, they believe, we can be in a better

position to adapt and aid people in their accomplishments. With more information, we can also balance ourselves on an interpersonal tightrope, crossing over between people's likes and dislikes, avoiding alienation.

In doing this, it's important not to make commitments too prematurely. It's important first to get the lay of the land, to take a pulse, a census, before taking action.

With Adapting-Dealing, it's be flexible, adapt, and fit in. "When in Rome, do as the Romans do," their saying goes. Knowing people and being in the know adds to our usefulness and our chance to get what we want.

Maintaining harmonious relationships also gets us what we want. This is the central issue: Getting along by keeping relationships running smoothly. Tact and diplomacy come to the forefront then. Empathy is the by-product, and we learn to sense what will win approval or lose it.

When talking to people whose plan is Adapting-Dealing, they insist, "Keep the peace, when you can. Whenever there's trouble, you have to calm the troubled waters. What's more important than getting along? You have to like people and people have to like you. That's what it's all about. You have to give and take. Live and let live. Life's too short for anything else."

Many times people who express the Adapting-Dealing orientation find it difficult to communicate their needs. When they do, their tact boomerangs. In an effort to avoid alienating the other person, they often fail in communicating.

They try to lighten up their requests with such tact and humor that the impact of their statements is neutralized by their pleasantries. In effect, their message is unrecognized. They are not taken seriously because they do not sound serious. Their light touch, their humor, distracts from the seriousness of their need and dissipates their impact.

With the Adapting-Dealing orientation, the person who pleases now feels that the person who receives the pleasure "owes him one." There's a private ledger "kept" on which all credits for pleasing are recorded. "Since I did something for you, now it's your turn to do something for me." It's quid pro quo, something for something. It's taking turns, only you come first.

When the person who follows the Adapting-Dealing path finally asks for something and is turned down, they can feel hurt and angry because their markers were not honored, the debt wasn't paid off. Often the recipient of the pleasing is unaware that the other person is keeping score and has an expectation that the marker will be acknowledged.

When it comes to planning and problem solving, the flexibility of Adapting-Dealing becomes very useful. People who prefer Adapting-Dealing can provide a willingness to entertain options and seek alternatives. Because of this, there is less vested interest in one's holding onto one position.

There is less need to save face, and people don't feel they are backing down or selling out. It's easier to compromise in the best sense of the word. An atmosphere is created in which everyone can more easily give and take, and so negotiate a solution that is satisfactory to the largest number of people.

With the desire for a quick resolution of differences, Adapting-Dealing can have a leavening effect on a group, smooth things out and help reestablish an atmosphere of give and take. With effective compromise, people can often go away from a conflict situation feeling everybody has gained something. Everybody has won. There are no losers.

Below is a summary of some of the strengths of Adapting-Dealing.
- Getting others excited about new ideas and keeping interest up in old ones.
- Adopting goals and facilitating others.
- Keeping in touch with people's thoughts and feelings.
- Using the light touch and taking the strain out of serious situations.
- Demonstrating flexibility and making workable compromises.

The name of the game is Harmony. Be flexible, fit in, adapt to what people need and want. Then you can ask for yours.

When people fully realize and act upon their most preferred orientations, they are satisfied because they use their strengths. When they are restrained from this, or when they are required to use their least preferred orientations, they experience dissatisfaction. They are fearful that they cannot be themselves, that they cannot use their strengths to cope.

No matter which of the four orientations is described, people have associations with them. When a description happens to be their most preferred orientation, they relate to it positively. They say, "Oh yes, of course! How else could you be?" And those people who have that particular orientation as their *least* preferred way say, "How in the world can anybody get by having that kind of philosophy?" The descriptions bring about strong feelings, value judgments about the "right" way to go through the world, the way that works best—"my way."

People usually look at their behavior from a qualitative point of view, a judgment of good or bad, right or wrong. In Life Orientations theory, people look at their behavior in a quantitative way, without judgment—not good or bad, right or wrong, but *more or less, most and least preferred.*

We need to learn to communicate with people in a more non-judgmental way. We need to say we are just different, not better or worse. Just different. This is one of the most rewarding results of the Life Orientations model.

5

TYPECASTING

LOOK BEHIND THE NAME

If you have decided upon which orientation you base your actions, I suggest that you think of yourself first as being a *mixture* of all of them. You are not one thing *or* another. You are one thing *and* another. Most of us have several orientations that we prefer most and one we prefer least.

Please don't put a label on yourself as a Supporter-Giver, or a Controller-Taker, Conserver-Holder, or Adapter-Dealer. The "er" connotes permanence. While there are hard and fixed labels, there are few hard and fixed people.

We are not the same all the time. That's why I selected the "ing" suffix in Supporting-Giving, Controlling-Taking, Conserving-Holding, and Adapting-Dealing. The "ing" suffix indicates an *action* or *process*.

The trouble with typologies or classification systems is that the labels wind up making people feel boxed in, typecast, judged. I do not want to classify people, I want to classify their *orientations, goals* and *actions*—their strengths and preferences to act one way or another under varying circumstances.

An American artist and student of Bhuddism, recently back from Tibet, reviewed my work. She said, "Some of these labels are so hard. The image I get is of rocks. Couldn't you find soft words for Controlling-Taking?" (Her preferences were Supporting-Giving and Adapting-Dealing.)

The semanticists tell us that the words are not hard. Words are words—neutral. Our meanings make them hard or soft. However, we do think in hard terms, and we are product-oriented. We want our products labeled clearly for instant recognition and evaluation.

The easiest course seems to be communication through labeling. It's easier to label a package or a person and believe the label tells us everything we need to know. It's easy to say that a person *is* an alcoholic, bed wetter, loudmouth, martyr, loser, primadonna. Conveniently, we get a picture. The trouble is that it is a freeze-frame and we forget to turn the camera back on. The label evokes permanent images.

The "is" is the villain. "Is" connotes an equal sign. For example, we might say that a person is a loudmouth. Person =loudmouth. More completely, we could say that this person is a person who experiences anxiety in a variety of situations and may dominate the conversation in varying degrees. They do this in order to make sure their ideas and desires are heard. They may talk so long and so loud that they alienate us. Our resentment rides out on the vehicle of the convenient label "loudmouth," because it feels so good to call names! But we could also say that if the person received assurance from us that we would hear their ideas and desires, meet their needs, then they might talk less and listen more. If we label them as a loudmouth, it stops us from thinking, and we will overlook alternatives or actions that could be helpful to reduce their tension.

It requires much more effort to look beyond the label, to experience the person as a dynamic process, to look at the fine print on the box and carefully study the ingredients inside the package. We have been conditioned to trust the label and look no further.

So labels are not only a shortcut, but they can be loaded as ammunition for resentment or distancing, for keeping us away from those strange creatures with the strange names, those inferior products.

We are what we think. I am suggesting that we think of people's complexity in a simple way. Think in terms of more or less, of sometimes this, other times that, of most preferred to least preferred. To think quantitatively like this is important as an antidote to the qualitative thinking of good or bad, right or wrong, strong or weak.

In thinking about ourselves quantitatively, we know that difficulty can follow our efforts if we do "too little" or "too much." What is needed is "just enough." To visualize this, we can look at the symbol of infinity. Not only does this symbolize, for me, the quantitative flow of our strengths, but it symbolizes the infinite possibilities for managing our strengths.

THE INFINITE FLOW OF OUR STRENGTHS

Least Preferred   *Most Preferred*
Strengths   *Strengths*

TOO LITTLE ◄——JUST ENOUGH——► TOO MUCH

DO MORE OF   DO LESS OF

Think in terms of "How Much." How much is enough? How much *more* can we use our *least* preferred strengths to add to our total power and perspective? How much *less* can we use our *most* preferred strengths to prevent self-defeating and alienating excess?

If we think "how much," improvement is possible without changing ourselves, without trying to be someone other people want us to be. We need only to control the *amount* of our strengths. A little more of this, a little less of that, until we hit the "just enough" position.

Thinking quantitatively can keep us reacting more positively to the ever-moving, ever-changing possibilities of people. Seeing the flow of strengths on the horizontal figure-eight can help counteract the judgment of fixed labels that over-simplify.

Gardner Murphy, the psychologist, in a book called *Outgrowing Self-Deception,* says, "Labeling and oversimplification is an escape from the reality of our inadequacies." Clearly, he says, if we didn't simplify by selecting what we see, we would be overwhelmed by all that is going on in our world and inside the worlds of other people. The effort it would take to deal with what is really there would be enormous. People therefore seek out the simple because it is more manageable.

Murphy concludes, "Soon the simple becomes boring and there's the excitement and exhilaration of *progressive mastery* of the complex. But people have to be led from the simple to the complex."

Though starting with simple labels, I have progressed to a more complex understanding of ourselves and our exchanges with people. Life Orientations theory has simple guidelines for improving complex human problems.

People are like a kaleidoscope, with twirling and twisting patterns, shapes and colors. Stop the kaleidoscope and you see one pattern. Turn it and there's a different one. The kaleidoscope contains the same pieces and colors and shapes, but with a quarter turn to the right or to the left, they reform into new patterns. Though people are in flux, their actions do have organization and patterning.

In some typologies people are put into hard and fixed categories—introverted or extroverted, dominant or submissive, subjective or objective. The basic position in Life Orientations theory is that we can be *all* of these things—a mix. Using a Life Orientations Survey, we clearly see the unique patterning of preferences.

Most of us have more than one preferred orientation, or more than one set of strengths. In two nationwide samples—one completed recently—of over 3,000 men and women in various vocations and professions, only nine percent have one main choice. With five percent, all four orientations are used uniformly.

Fifteen percent have three orientations that are about equal in preference, while the fourth one is preferred much less. Fifty-five percent have two orientations that guide their lives.

Finally, sixteen percent of the people we analyzed had a strong preference for one orientation, with two others equally strong as a back-up.

LIFE ORIENTATIONS SURVEY RESULTS

90 Points are distributed over the Four Orientations.

SG—Supporting-Giving   CH—Conserving-Holding
CT—Controlling-Taking   AD—Adapting-Dealing

The Six Basic Patterns

FOUR MAIN CHOICES:

(Frequency—5%)

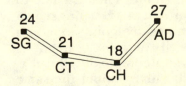

ONE MAIN AND ONE BACK-UP CHOICE:
(Frequency—24%)

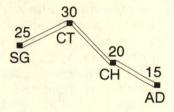

ONE MAIN CHOICE:

(Frequency—9%)

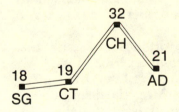

ONE MAIN CHOICE AND TWO SECOND CHOICES:
(Frequency—16%)

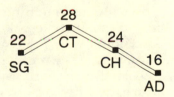

TWO MAIN CHOICES:
(Frequency—31%)

THREE MAIN CHOICES:
(Frequency—15%)

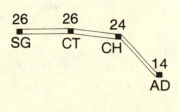

Time and time again, the results of the Life Orientations Survey have indicated that we are not just one thing or another. It is inaccurate to typecast. We are complex and dynamic. Yet, there must be a way to stop the kaleidoscope and look at our patterning, the unique mix of shapes, colors and forms that make up our lives. To make some sense out of ourselves and others, to simplify our complexity, we need a common language, a common frame of reference. We need to think about ourselves in a systematic and organized way.

Focusing on the four orientations to life accomplishes this need for simplicity and structure. The structure is limited to four orientations because it's more manageable. Practically, we can only handle a certain number of concepts at one time. If we created ten or twelve orientations, it would be so unmanageable that we would not be able to use the information and apply the ideas.

After looking at other classification systems, my conclusion about the orientations is that Supporting-Giving, Controlling-Taking, Conserving-Holding and Adapting-Dealing are such composite categories that each seems to be an umbrella big enough for large numbers of people to get under comfortably.

This is what psychologist George Kelly called the mini-max theory. Personal constructs to explain our actions should follow a rule: the minimum number of categories to cover the maximum number of events.

Some people ask, "Well, four orientations, isn't that oversimplifying life? We're more complex than that." My answer is, "Yes, we are complex, and so is Life Orientations theory. But it starts simply by identifying the name of our game, and it progresses to provide structured guidelines for complex problems."

Even though there are only four categories, more complexity evolves because they can be arranged in a pattern, a mix, a first, second, third, and fourth choice. This happens when we survey people's orientations to life. They are able to pattern their preferences for the four orientations under two sets of conditions; *favorable*—when things are going well, and *adverse*—when things are not going well. With four categories under *two sets of conditions,* there is more complexity. But it is still manageable, because we are still talking about the same basic Four.

When preferences are indicated on the LIFO survey, a point value results with each category ranging from 9 to 36. This leads to another level of complexity within the simplicity of the Four. For example, you could have Controlling-Taking as your most preferred choice, and that could be a point value of 34, and I could also have Controlling-Taking as my most preferred way, but the point value could be 28. We could be different in the relative intensity of our preferences.

There is another way we could be different within our similarity. If we both have Controlling-Taking as our main choice, you could have Supporting-Giving as your second choice, and I could have Conserving-Holding as my second choice. We could be different in second choices, but similar with our first.

Statistically, the possibilities for complexity astound me. For example, ranking our preferences for the four orientations under two conditions—favorable and adverse—results in a mix of eight categories. These eight can be likened to the eight notes on a musical scale. They can be arranged in many different patterns. As in music, they could result in a simple folk song or a complex symphony. It only takes eight notes. So it is with the survey results. While there are only eight categories to be ranked, the point value of each category can range from 9 to 36. This yields a possible 22,400 patterns!

While we are all using the same eight "notes" to orchestrate our lives, the music that comes out is not the same, and the concert halls in which we play vary. How marvelous it is that we can be so similar *and* so different, so simple *and* so complex.

The meaning behind Life Orientations theory is complex, but it suggests a simple, finite framework which helps us cope with the infinite.

We simplify the complex by working only with our *most* preferred and our *least* preferred orientations. Yet, these two dimensions tell us a great deal about how we can be more productive personally, how to help others to be more productive, and how we can communicate together more effectively.

6

OVERPLAYING OUR GAME

TOO MUCH OF A GOOD THING

Our so-called weaknesses are nothing more than strengths pushed to an excess. Confidence turns into arrogance, flexibility turns into inconsistency, trust turns into gullibility, and analysis turns into paralysis.

We exaggerate our strengths to excess under two entirely different conditions. These conditions are favorable and adverse—when things are going well, and when they are not going well.

Under favorable conditions, excess occurs because we enjoy our strengths and look for every opportunity to use them. They give us satisfaction and pleasure. We feel like our true selves, doing what comes naturally. We may be involved in excelling, getting results, using our heads, or in seeking harmony. That's us. We love it! Why not do as much of it as possible?

Ah, but gluttony is our undoing. There can be too much of a good thing, and our pleasure can be someone else's displeasure. Others can sense the self-serving nature of our efforts and feel put upon, and react negatively to stop us. What's more, perhaps the task at hand does not require that degree of excellence, that quick an action, or that much analysis, or that much concern about harmony.

Time, effort and money can be wasted while we overuse our strengths for our own purpose—self-pleasure.

If our preference is Supporting-Giving, we can be delighted at any opportunity to help someone in need, or we can be happy trying harder when things do not go right, or we can jump in to rescue other people at the slightest sign of need. While these inclinations are admirable, we can become overcommitted helping others, to the neglect of our own needs, and to the neglect of other people who should be our priority. Instead of taking the responsibility for always trying harder to make things right, other people should be given the responsibility for doing their fair share! Trying harder may be a waste of effort if reason is called for. It might be better to work smarter, not harder.

Controlling-Taking excess is different. We can be so captivated by the challenge of a difficult situation that we persist just to prove we can master and overcome the difficulty. Overcoming is the pleasure, showing ourselves and others we can do it is the self-reward, notwithstanding the time, effort and money it may have cost to get the results. Say it can't be done, and we'll show you it can.

With Conserving-Holding, the strength of precision, and accuracy and completeness can lead to analysis-paralysis and over-elaborate use of information. Ask for the time of day and we'll give you a dissertation on how the watch works.

In our desire for harmony and getting along, the excess with Adapting-Dealing can slip into placating others and forgetting our own course and preferences. If too many people are involved in a situation, we may be pulled every which way, from pillar to post trying to please them all, and suffer the confusion of trying to be "all things to all men."

How much of a good thing is enough? That's a very subjective question, and varies with the people with whom we are associating, and from situation to situation. Nevertheless, the optimum use of our strengths is possible. We can learn over a period of time how much is enough, so that other people are not frustrated with us, and so we don't sacrifice effectiveness for undue satisfaction.

Back in the 5th Century, B.C., the Chinese sage Lao Tzu said it best in the classic book *Tao Te Ching* (pronounced "Dow Da Ching"). In Chapter IX, he says, "Over-sharpen the blade and the edge will soon blunt." And speaking of excess more generally, he said, "More is less, and less is more." Ironically, the more strength we use, the less effective it is, and the less strength used, the more effective.

When I bought my daughters their first bicycles, I was quite concerned for their safety. Following the instructions for assembly, I carefully placed the front wheel in the front frame and threaded a nut on each end of the axle-bolt that goes through the wheel. Now, the instructions said tighten the nuts by hand until they won't turn, and then take a wrench and tighten the nut one-quarter turn clockwise. "Well," said I, "if a quarter turn is good, a full turn must be better." Snap! The thread stripped as I made my full turn. Too much strength.

Stereo fans know there is an optimum volume. Turn up the system too loud, and it is a strain, and distortion sets in.

Every salad maker among us knows that the cold, crisp vegetables are enhanced by a delicious dressing. But put in too much dressing and it overpowers the flavor of the vegetables—and the salad gets soggy.

Baseball pitchers understand this principle well. The slider is a fast ball that slides down and away. If you throw it too hard, it stays straight and doesn't slide away. Just the right amount of strength is required. A plant will die if it doesn't get sufficient water. Put in too much water and the new delicate roots will rot, and the plant dies from too much of what it needs to live.

Take in too much oxygen and we will hyperventilate. Too little oxygen and it's goodbye.

All life is a balance between too little and too much.

Looking at some of the strengths of each orientation in the tables below, we can see the inevitable extension of using our strengths too much.

SUPPORTING-GIVING ORIENTATION

STRENGTH	EXCESS
Thoughtful	Self-Denying
Idealistic	Utopian
Modest	Self-Effacing
Trusting	Gullible
Loyal	Blindly Allegiant
Cooperative	Passive
Helpful	Overprotective

CONTROLLING-TAKING ORIENTATION

STRENGTH	*EXCESS*
Confident	Arrogant
Forceful	Coercive
Quick	Impulsive
Competitive	Combative
Active	Impatient
Directing	Domineering
Enterprising	Opportunistic

CONSERVING-HOLDING ORIENTATION

STRENGTH	*EXCESS*
Methodical	Plodding
Tenacious	Stubborn
Thrifty	Stingy
Reserved	Withdrawn
Practical	Unimaginative
Systematic	Complicated
Factual	Data-Bound

ADAPTING-DEALING ORIENTATION

STRENGTH	*EXCESS*
Tactful	Placating
Enthusiastic	Fervent
Negotiating	Yielding
Experimental	Aimless
Humorous	Foolish
Flexible	Acquiescent
Eager	Childish

To prevent these excesses, we need to moderate our strengths. We need to become aware first, and then gear back, *do less of,* in order to be more effective. This does not mean we have to change ourselves. On the contrary, we need only to take a little something off our pitch, modulate our volume, to reach the threshold where our so-called weaknesses are considered strengths.

To keep ourselves in the strength zone, and prevent ourselves from crossing over into excess, is not an easy matter. We need to learn that we can give other people permission to point out when we're going into overkill. Someone else can see it more clearly. If we give them permission to watch us from the sidelines, they can keep us from giving too much, coming on too strong, holding on too long, or pleasing too many.

Ordinarily, we do not think in terms of strength and excess side by side. We think in terms of right and wrong, good or bad, strength or weakness. This polar thinking keeps us from seeing how our actions are a matter of degree, more or less, a position between two poles.

Our daily language is also inadequate to describe our action by degrees. The dictionary is filled with adjectives that describe our characteristics, but they are scattered alphabetically. We find no order here. We cannot see the phenomenon of strengths *sliding into* excess, the productive becoming counter-productive.

We are trusting or gullible, quick or impulsive, methodical or plodding, flexible or acquiescent. Where are the words to describe us *between* those extremes, words that might give us clues or warning signals that we are approaching the excess? Those words are few and far between. An examination of a thesaurus or a dictionary is disheartening when we look for words to describe human behavior by degrees. Here are some possibilities listed in the tables below.

SUPPORTING-GIVING ORIENTATION

STRENGTH	THRESHOLD	EXCESS
Thoughtful	Indulging	Self-Denying
Idealistic	Impractical	Utopian
Modest	Deferring	Self-Effacing
Trusting	Guileless	Gullible
Loyal	Devoted	Blindly Allegiant
Cooperative	Compliant	Passive
Helpful	Parental	Overprotective

CONTROLLING-TAKING ORIENTATION

STRENGTH	THRESHOLD	EXCESS
Confident	Cocky	Arrogant
Forceful	Insistent	Coercive
Quick	Hasty	Impulsive
Competitive	Contentious	Combative
Active	Urgent	Impatient
Directing	Bossy	Domineering
Enterprising	Changing	Opportunistic

CONSERVING-HOLDING ORIENTATION

STRENGTH	THRESHOLD	EXCESS
Methodical	Painstaking	Plodding
Tenacious	Unyielding	Stubborn
Thrifty	Sparing	Stingy
Reserved	Aloof	Withdrawn
Practical	Utilitarian	Unimaginative
Systematic	Elaborate	Complicated
Factual	Concrete	Data-Bound

ADAPTING-DEALING ORIENTATION

STRENGTH	THRESHOLD	EXCESS
Tactful	Solicitous	Placating
Enthusiastic	Excitable	Fervent
Humorous	Silly	Foolish
Negotiating	Vacillating	Yielding
Experimental	Drifting	Aimless
Flexible	Impressionable	Acquiescent
Eager	Flighty	Childish

No doubt our behavior varies in these intensities. There is a middle ground before excess. But it is difficult to detect in the rush of daily life. For all practical purposes, we don't realize that we are in excess until we are there, and other people tell us.

. The following table shows how we view each other's excesses and how this impacts our relationships.

THE IMPACT OF EXCESSI

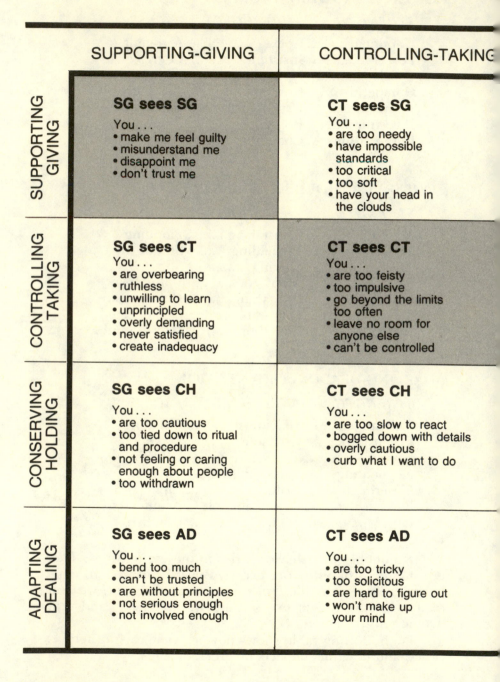

	SUPPORTING-GIVING	CONTROLLING-TAKING

SUPPORTING GIVING	**SG sees SG**
	You . . .
	• make me feel guilty
	• misunderstand me
	• disappoint me
	• don't trust me
		CT sees SG
		You . . .
		• are too needy
		• have impossible
		  standards
		• too critical
		• too soft
		• have your head in
		  the clouds

CONTROLLING TAKING	**SG sees CT**
	You . . .
	• are overbearing
	• ruthless
	• unwilling to learn
	• unprincipled
	• overly demanding
	• never satisfied
	• create inadequacy
		CT sees CT
		You . . .
		• are too feisty
		• too impulsive
		• go beyond the limits
		  too often
		• leave no room for
		  anyone else
		• can't be controlled

CONSERVING HOLDING	**SG sees CH**
	You . . .
	• are too cautious
	• too tied down to ritual
	  and procedure
	• not feeling or caring
	  enough about people
	• too withdrawn
		CT sees CH
		You . . .
		• are too slow to react
		• bogged down with details
		• overly cautious
		• curb what I want to do

ADAPTING DEALING	**SG sees AD** You . . . • bend too much • can't be trusted • are without principles • not serious enough • not involved enough	**CT sees AD** You . . . • are too tricky • too solicitous • are hard to figure out • won't make up your mind

N EACH OTHER

CONSERVING-HOLDING	ADAPTING-DEALING	
CH sees SG You . . . • are too emotional • not objective enough • need to be more consistent and practical	**AD sees SG** You . . . • are too serious • too pious • too critical	SUPPORTING GIVING
CH sees CT You . . . • are too impulsive • too emotional • possibly dangerous • disregard costs and practical issues	**AD sees CT** You . . . • are not heedful enough of people's reactions • are locked in too much to your own point of view • don't tune in enough to others	CONTROLLING TAKING
CH sees CH You . . . • are too precise • too factual • are locked into only one set of data	**AD sees CH** You . . . • are too serious • don't have enough regard for people's feelings • too rigid and unbending	CONSERVING HOLDING
CH sees AD You . . . • are too people-oriented • not practical enough • joke around too much • disregard rules	**AD sees AD** You . . . • fake me out too often • make me feel like I've been fooled • make me feel uneasy with all the promises	ADAPTING DEALING

Notice the diagonal squares where the same orientations meet each other. These descriptions are softer and more forgiving than those of two different orientations. It seems we are more tolerant and understanding with people who are like us, who share our excess.

Yet it is through working and communicating with people who are different from us that the possibility for controlling our excess clearly rests. Making use of their differences as a control, a check and balance, can keep us from over-using our strengths in the first place. Differences ultimately can neutralize excess.

If we are Supporting-Giving and at times tend to aim too high, be too idealistic, wouldn't it be useful to be counterbalanced by someone who is practical and down to earth?

If we are Controlling-Taking and at times tend to move too fast, be too active, wouldn't it help us to be supplemented by someone who could slow us down and make us think twice before we act?

If we are Conserving-Holding and at times tend to move too slowly, be too cautious, wouldn't it get us going to work with someone who could light a fire under us?

And finally, if we are Adapting-Dealing and at times tend to stay too loose, be too flexible, wouldn't it give us clearer direction to be with someone who could stand on his or her convictions and keep us on the straight and narrow? We do need each other for many reasons, not the least of which is the necessity for controlling excesses.

Now let's consider the excess under adverse conditions, when things are not going well. Under adverse conditions, excess takes on a completely different character. Here the excess is not a blithe and blind extension of our strength. It is not for our fun and self-satisfaction. On the contrary, it is summoned to fight our battles and cope with the emergencies that confront us in times of stress and high pressure. Adverse conditions also include times when people strongly disagree with us, or when they actively oppose what we want to accomplish.

Adverse conditions set off alarm bells in us. At times like these, our autonomic nervous system takes over. Our body mobilizes its forces. We jump to the ready. We're in red alert. We become the fighter pilot, buttoning our last piece of gear as we scramble across the air strip and pull ourselves into the cockpit. We become the fireman, tugging up our boots, sliding down the pole, and jumping onto the fire truck as it pulls out of the fire station.

What we face under the pressure in our own lives may not be as dramatic as what the fighter pilot or the fireman faces, but what goes on inside our bodies is just the same.

Hans Selye, the "father" of stress research, first identified what happens to us under stress back in 1937 in his book *The Stress of Life*. He called our stress reactions the General Adaptation Syndrome (G.A.S.). It is simply a series of steps or stages we all experience after our alarm bells go off.

Selye called the first stage of adaptation to stress ... Alarm. Any situation or action by another person which is perceived by us as threatening our physical or psychological well-being triggers the alarm. Our primitive brain, the hypothalamus, signals our body to get ready to act, and we respond with all sorts of physical reactions. For example, our heart beats quicker, hormones in our blood send sugar to the muscles and brain for full energy, and our breathing quickens to take in more oxygen. We sweat or go cold. We get "hot under the collar," or get "cold feet."

Depending upon the nature and seriousness of the threat, we can rise to the occasion quickly. We handle the disagreement or deal with the emergency. The threat is now gone. Our body returns to a state of equilibrium. We've coped. We are back in favorable conditions.

But if we don't cope with the adversity, the threat continues. In this case, we can enter the second stage of adapting to stress ... Saturation.

This means that our bodily reactions continue at a high level to keep us in a defensive state. Our muscles can stay tense, heart rate stays quickened, blood pressure remains high, and the hormones in our blood keep sending sugar to our muscles and brain for full energy. We take our exaggerated effort for granted. But we are borrowing from the future. We are so busy dealing with the stress or conflict that we no longer notice our bodily reactions. It feels like second nature. We're up. Alert. Haven't we always been this way?

If the stress continues uncorrected, our sharpened edge of awareness and effort may blunt. We begin to feel inadequate. We feel frustrated or angry, perhaps depressed.

What follows is the feeling of *distress.* Unrelieved stress piled on stress can lead to distress, says Hans Seyle. Stress stimulates, but distress debilitates.

Enter excess. "Well," we say to ourselves, "since our efforts are failing and we're feeling distress, why not use more of our strengths?" So we reach into our reserve energy bank and put something extra into our efforts. The something extra is usually excess.

For example, in the Supporting-Giving orientation under stress, there is a willingness to assume responsibility, take the blame, and to try to do it better by working harder or longer hours. While this often effectively copes with stress, it can also lead to the excess of becoming critical of one's self and others when the impossible can't be achieved. When things are not going well, we say that it's up to us to do better. "Good" people "ought to" be able to do it.

Under stress, with a Controlling-Taking orientation, we can cope effectively by being quick to respond with intensified effort. With a sense of urgency, we can deal with many problems on several fronts simultaneously. But this runs the risk of diffusing our efforts, by running ourselves ragged and acting unilaterally instead of checking things with the other people involved. Our urgency can exaggerate to emergency, throwing others into a feeling of panic.

Conserving-Holding under stress copes by analyzing alternatives and setting priorities in a level-headed way, approaching the problem systematically. Exaggerate this to excess and we have analysis-paralysis, decision deadlines missed, and the hazards and urgency in the situation ignored, as if we have all the time in the world.

With Adapting-Dealing, stress is frequently handled by striving to keep tension low, getting things done through humor, and smoothing things out with reassuring promises and a positive outlook. The other side of this, the excess, is that we distract from the seriousness of the situation and may raise hopes too high, disappointing others if things don't work out.

It is in the second stage of adapting to stress, when we are saturated and numbed to our distressful condition, that excess has the greatest opportunity to activate. We are not turning things around. We are blocked. We feel vulnerable. The obvious solution is to go to more of our strengths. But this can boomerang and create a counter-productive excess *adding* to the distress!

If the emergency doesn't stop, if the threat persists without relief, we go into the third stage of adaptation... Exhaustion. Suddenly, we burn out. It seems to have come out of nowhere. We don't feel that we can do one more thing. Crash. Time for R and R, or martinis, a vacation, some mindless hours in front of TV, or sex—if we have the energy, or if we can arouse the feeling side of ourselves.

It is in this final stage of exhaustion that we finally have a clue that we have been under distress. This realization can come after one hour, one day, one month or one year!

Whether one hour or one year, it is too long. Most likely, we have alienated some important people, wasted time and effort, and have abused our bodies.

But not all stress is harmful. It can be exhilarating. Many of us do our best work, perform at top levels, under stress. It is only after distress and excess emerge that stress is counter-productive.

What is stressful for me, however, may not be stressful for you. Different things set us off. Our alarms may be very different, or the same alarm may have to be clanged longer and louder for one of us to hear it.

But what are these alarms? And what can we do about them to avoid excess, or stop them once they start?

First the alarms. There are eight alarms caused by what's happening in the situation. There are also eight personal alarms that are built into us and which we take with us wherever we go, irrespective of what's happening in the situation.

Situationally, the alarms are:

- Unrealisitic deadlines.
- Vague objectives.
- Unclear lines of authority and responsibility.
- Non-support from key people upon whom we must rely.
- Contradictory expectations from at least two key people pulling in opposite directions.
- Increased responsibility over people or dollars.
- Overload from the amount to be done, or from the lack of experience in doing it.
- Changes happening too fast, or too slow.

Personal alarms are:

- Fear of failure, or actually failing.
- Invasion of our territory, real or anticipated.
- High risk decisions.
- Unfamiliar situations.
- Fear of being deprived of what we need, or actual deprivation.
- Perceived attack on our self-esteem and integrity.
- Resistance and opposition to what we want to accomplish.
- Competition or rivalry to win or lose, be right or wrong.

The alarms are everywhere. Which ones send you into the alarm state of stress? Which alarms make you vulnerable to stress and excess?

If you can't identify them, you need to be more aware and vigilant. If you are already numbed by the alarms, you don't have to wait for the final stage of exhaustion to alert yourself that you have been in distress.

Fortunately, our excess is an *early warning signal* of trouble, *before* any physical by-products of distress are produced. Our excess, the exaggerated use of our strengths, is in itself a distress signal, as visible as a distress flare in darkness, lighting up the sky. If we pay attention to our excess, then we have accomplished a major step in managing our stress.

After spotting our excess as a distress signal, we need to gear back. We need to identify the alarms *within* ourselves or *around* us in the situation, or both. We need to face the factors that are creating the stress in the first place.

If it's the *rapid rate of changes* in our lives, we need to slow the rate of change, or space out the changes over a longer period of time.

If we experience ourselves at *high risk,* we need to own up to it and restructure the situation and our activities to be less risky.

If *vague objectives* have us hazy about our direction and are creating uneasiness and uncertainty, then we need to focus with key people about our direction and set some clearly attainable and measurable goals.

If *fear of failure, invasion of our territory, competition or rivalry* are the alarms, we need to do some reconditioning and re-education to desensitize ourselves to the emotional effects of the alarms. This may take time and could require some coaching or counseling from someone we trust.

It is more productive to problem-solve and restructure our situation, or to desensitize ourselves to the personal alarms, than to keep attacking our stress with an exaggerated and counter-productive effort. Excess creates more excess; it's cyclical. To stop the excess, we cannot simply reprimand ourselves that we are being self-righteous, arrogant, nitpicky or placating. Instead of emotionally scolding ourselves for being "bad," we must attack the source of the stress, be it in the situation or in us—or both.

Nor does being scolded by others alleviate the problem. It does little good to be called "outrageous," "thoughtless," or "selfish." Being corrected, criticized or ostracized doesn't change the *source* of our stress. It only adds to our feelings of inadequacy and frustration, and it creates more excess!

Ultimatums that demand we shape up or lose our key relationships do not help either. They only add to the agony and alienation. Ignorance about distress and excess is the enemy.

Correct the source of stress through problem-solving, shut off those situational and personal alarms—then our excess will fall silent, along with the distress.

Now, while we are in the process of correcting the source of stress, we may want to alleviate some of our distress through the meditation or relaxation techniques that are growing in popularity. Or, we may seek a medical solution if some physical symptoms have erupted.

But remember, first things first. The medical approach to stress is *after-the-fact,* when our body finally gives way. Relaxation is a *during-the-fact* remedy to subdue the body's severe reactions to the stress. Managing our strengths and excesses is a *before-the-fact* approach that goes to the source of the problem to reduce or eliminate the causes of stress.

As if all the forces *outside* ourselves weren't sufficient source of stress, we create our own—even when things go well. Stress can be *self-induced,* quietly, imperceptibly. We can slip beyond our productive ways into excess when there are no alarms, no stressful conditions, just our own inner desire to meet the goals of our orientations. In our effort to follow our orientations, in pursuit of a more meaningful life, we strive to meet the goals of our game plan. Our striving can lead to stress and distress when we go overboard trying to be who we are.

If we are Supporting-Giving, we push ourselves to excel, to try harder, to give. If we are Controlling-Taking, we press ourselves to overcome challenges, to do more, to seize every opportunity, large or small. If we are Conserving-Holding, we exert ourselves to be accurate, to be complete, to preserve what we have. If we are Adapting-Dealing, we extend ourselves to get along, to keep everybody happy, to avoid conflict.

We need to control our excess, even when there is no threat, when there are no alarms. We need to watch and be watched. We need our trusted friends, loved ones, and trusted co-workers to remind us that we are giving, doing, holding, or adapting beyond the call of duty, beyond the real needs of the people and the situation which confronts us. We need people who are different from us to be our check and balance. And we need to learn to use our least preferred orientations more, as our own counterbalancing force against excess.

The energy that goes into excess, the stress it creates, is enough to exhaust a nation.

We need to moderate the strengths of our orientations, to orchestrate them as a rich source of new possibilities for better health, increased satisfaction, and greater productivity in our lives.

7

THE CASE
OF THE APOLOGETIC
EXECUTIVE

Alex, a top executive from a client company, telephoned me, and he sounded tense. His uncharacteristic seriousness warned me that he felt troubled. "I have to get my act together," Alex said in a somewhat foreboding way. "I'd like to talk with you." I could hear the distress in his voice. I cleared my schedule to see him at his office the next morning.

Before I saw Alex, I had occasion to talk to his boss, the company president. I asked him if he knew of any crisis going on with Alex. He knew nothing, but he was glad Alex was using me as a resource.

In Alex's office, I sat down among the working clutter and the memorabilia. His face was tight, drawn, not the usual half-smiling face that made it difficult to tell if he was feeling good or bad. Alex said that he was seeking my opinion on whether he was right or wrong. Certain recent events in the company, with himself as central protagonist, were disturbing him.

Here is his story. For several years, a competitor had won a sizeable amount of business from a mutual customer. Alex's division could have supplied the customer with the product, too. But there was one major obstacle—price. The competition could sell it for twenty percent less. In Alex's company, the pricing committee—of which Alex was not a member—had calculated the price which made him lose out to the competition.

Alex had taken some kidding about not getting that business for his division, from both people in the industry and from inside the company. Getting that business was important because the company had never sold that type of product before, and it could have opened up a new market, accounting for millions of dollars.

Finally, on a dare from the chairman of the board, Alex felt that he had been given an unofficial mandate to get the new business, despite the pricing committee's roadblock. Problem number one was the pricing. Problem number two was that the president of the company had final authority over the pricing committee's recommendations.

Problem number three was that the president and Alex were not close. In fact, from Alex's point of view, the president did not like him, and he, Alex, said that he would give anything to know how to win over the president and please him.

Alex had respect for the president's authority and ability, but he felt that the president always wanted to be right, seldom admitting mistakes. He had felt this stress of not being liked by the president for the past ten years, but in the present circumstances it had become acute.

This is why the problem came to a head. Unilaterally and unofficially, Alex investigated the cost figures and other factors that the pricing committee reviewed, and he came to a different conclusion. His calculations and pricing logic made the product's price more in line with the competition's. Though the price was still slightly higher than the competition's, Alex felt that he could justify the slightly higher price to the customer on the grounds of better performance and service.

Alex said that he checked his information sources again and did his calculations a second time to make sure. His homework was thorough and conclusive. He called his major customer that the competition had won over, and he quoted the new price to the customer that was lower than the original quote from the pricing committee.

The customer was delighted because he had wanted before to place the business with Alex, but couldn't justify the size of the price discrepancy between Alex and his competition. The customer gave Alex a landmark order, with the promise of more. The purchase order arrived and was processed through channels.

Alex's telephone did not stop ringing. Congratulations came from many sources. The sales force saw it as a breakthrough for their selling efforts and their commission potential. But they could also hold their heads high again. When their major competition had beaten them out on the new product, it had also reflected unfavorably on their regular products.

Amid all the celebration, there was no word from the president. No telephone call, no memo. Only silence. Alex's anxiety swelled. Time passed. Two weeks later, the chief financial officer of the company dropped into Alex's office to discuss a memo he had received from the president. It read in part, "Regarding Alex's sale. The pricing committee is supposed to review it. Procedures?"

The financial executive wasn't quite sure of the intent behind the memo, and Alex didn't feel any more the wiser about how the president was taking the whole matter. After talking over Alex's calculations, the financial executive agreed that it seemed sound. Another week passed, and still no damnation or praise from the president.

Finally, Alex composed an interdepartmental memo *from* himself *to* himself. It was a full page, praising himself for his ingenuity and initiative in establishing this new class of business. In the salutation of the memo, he embellished his already impressive title to make it sound even more impressive.

After he read his memo from himself to himself, it sounded so good and so humorous, that he did one thing more. He sent out the memo with full distribution around the company.

People were delighted about his light touch to a touchy situation. Still no word from the president. Several days later, the head of administration and the head of personnel came to Alex's office. The president had questioned them about Alex's new title! They blustered and flustered about the need to keep titles uniform and keep title changes within existing policy. Alex explained that it was a joke, and that he would not be using that title anymore.

More time passed and finally Alex's stress was causing him sleepless nights. And to make matters worse, just when he was already in such an uncertain and tense state, another company had come to him and made him a very attractive job offer which sounded tempting.

I told Alex that I had listened very carefully and that I understood his feelings and his stress. I also said that I wanted to give him my impressions and reactions to the events, that I would suggest actions that he could take to reduce his stress. I also said I could give him some guidelines to improve his relationship with the president.

In my final preamble, I stated that what I said would focus on what's best for him, and how this, in the long run, would be best for the company. I emphasized that he could not control the company or the president, but that he could control his reactions and the meaning of the events. This could give him more focus and energy to deal with the situation.

Alex encouraged me to give my honest opinion—where he was right and where he was wrong. He wanted to know because he was confused. He reminded me that he had as good judgment as anybody—after all, he was number one in his graduation class at college. In effect, Alex was apologizing for his actions and trying to justify his position. I side-stepped the invitation to evaluate and judge him. I said that I would only identify and explain what I saw happening and what possible options he had in dealing with the situation to solve the problems in it. With those conditions clear, I gave my impressions.

First of all, I stated that I sensed that he was a person who valued the opinion other people had of him, that he liked to please. With the chairman of the board goading him to get the new business, it had put Alex in conflict with the president to whom he reported directly. Alex was in the middle. To please one would be to displease the other.

Because he was frustrated so long over non-competitive pricing, he probably welcomed the chairman's unofficial demand for action. Now Alex could say, "The Devil made me do it!" He now had support for his own long-suppressed inclinations. The secret crusade was to prove who was right and who was wrong. Alex smiled and said that the explanation hit it on the head.

But like most secrecy, I went on to explain, fear and guilt can be by-products, and so that made his feelings for the president more acute, supposing that the president's dislike would now magnify to wrath and punishment. What is more, he had set up a win or lose, right or wrong challenge between the pricing committee and himself, but his victory had brought more stress than he bargained for.

I also pointed out to Alex that he had no information about the president's opinion. In the absence of praise for his accomplishment, Alex assumed the opposite—severe criticism. I added that, from my point of view, he and the president had very different styles. I indicated to Alex that he was not seeing the possibility that the president was reacting in characteristic style to the situation, just as he, Alex was.

I emphasized to Alex that I knew, firsthand, that the president was not harboring severe criticism of the event or of Alex's actions. The upset had come from his end. Therefore, when no word came to him directly, he had filled in the void with his own anxiety, not knowing if the president was pleased or displeased with his unilateral action. Not being able to tolerate that ambiguity, he wrote the self-praising memo and sent it around the company—as a "joke."

That joke served a twofold purpose. One, it gave Alex the praise that he needed, and it might have precipitated some action on the part of the president to tell Alex where he stood—approved or disapproved.

But I explained further that the memo only called more attention to the deed, and if the president was hoping that the original incident would fade into the background, it was now in the spotlight. Conjecturing further, I told Alex that the president might have been dissatisfied with the committee's pricing conclusions, too, but did not want to overrule them. Suppose further that he was privately pleased that Alex took the leadership to challenge the committee. It was possible that the president did not see the cause of the situation as Alex's defiance against policy, but as Alex having the guts to go out on a limb to bring about necessary change.

Even if my explanations were not correct, I indicated that they still demonstrated that there were alternative interpretations beyond the president's not liking him. I also indicated that the reason for the distance could be the differences in their orientations.

Alex was still puzzled by the president's way of doing things, but much of his tension and stress seemed to have subsided. I recommended that we continue our discussion the following day for at least an hour and a half, at which time we could place particular emphasis on any differences in style between himself and the president. I said that it was important to look at what was happening more objectively, so that he could make a decision about leaving the company from choice, not from the compulsion to retaliate for his distress.

From my work with the president and from his results on the Life Orientations Survey, I knew that his most preferred orientation was Conserving-Holding. His constant lament was that he wanted his executives to do their homework, to think more systematically, and take the broad company viewpoint rather than their own departmental view. While he liked upbeat people with positive points of view, he did not like raw enthusiasm, unrestrained emotion, and a lack of serious intent. Business was serious business.

The president's second preference was the Controlling-Taking orientation. He did like action and advancement. He did like competition and winning, but he believed in building on what was unique about the company and preserving its identity at the risk of being inflexible at times.

But I had no information on Alex. From previous encounters and from our meeting, I took a guess that Alex's orientation was Adapting-Dealing. Alex was enthusiastic, emotional, eager, excitable, flexible, just the opposite of the president's more reserved, tenacious, and methodical approach.

The next day I went to see Alex again, and I brought Training workbooks with me to have him compare his orientations with the president's. It was 9 o'clock in the morning, and Alex came into his office looking surprisingly fresh and rested. Still in a deeply serious state, for him, Alex said that he had been called into the president's office after our meeting the day before. He and the president had discussed Alex's pricing formula and the possibilities for selling the new product to more customers. The president admitted that Alex might be right with the pricing and wanted him to become a permanent member of the pricing committee!

Alex conceded that the president's reactions to the situation were hopeful, but that the president was still an enigma to him. With that cue, I suggested that Alex take the Survey to identify his orientations and strengths. Then I said that I had permission from the president to share information on his preferences and strengths.

Alex's preferences turned out to be Adapting-Dealing first, Controlling-Taking second, Supporting-Giving third, and Conserving-Holding last! Alex's *least* preferred orientation was the president's *most* preferred. And the Adapting-Dealing orientation, which was Alex's first choice, was the president's last.

Following the sequence in the Training workbook, I first highlighted Alex's strengths, his unique contributions. Then we talked about his excesses. Then I contrasted Alex's strengths and excesses with the president's. The contrasts were revealing.

	THE PRESIDENT	ALEX
	Conserving-Holding	Adapting-Dealing
Strength	Relies heavily on data, analysis, and logic to make decisions.	Uses the light touch and personal charm to win over people.
Excess	May get too involved in data and fail to appreciate other people's lack of interest.	Becomes overly entertaining and distracts from the seriousness of the situation.
Strength	Methodical and consistently follows procedures or policies.	Flexible in finding ways to satisfy other people.
Excess	May not be flexible enough to provide concessions which would help solve a problem.	Can accommodate too much to people's wishes, switching sides on issues.

	THE PRESIDENT	ALEX
	Conserving-Holding	Adapting-Dealing
Strength	Can respond objectively and calmly to objections posed by others.	Strives to keep tension low through humor and smoothing over disagreement.
Excess	May not demonstrate enough feeling and concern, and may appear uninvolved.	May prevent objections from being fully expressed so that the problem re-occurs.
Strength	Sticks with procedures, policies, and well-tested ways.	Ready to change and adapt to new ideas and ways.
Excess	Gets stuck with old ways when a new approach may be helpful.	Seems aimless and unfocused, confusing others.

Their differences were striking, and they were an obvious source of difficulty and distancing. How could they feel close when they were so far apart?

Studying the contrasts began to relieve Alex's subjective feeling that the president somehow had singled him out as a target of rejection and displeasure. Because the differences were written and outlined objectively, they seemed less personally directed.

The events of the product pricing drama fell into place. The workbook statements gave form, shape, and retrospective meaning to the events. A new, more objective explanation of their relationship was coming about, demystifying and diffusing the emotionally charged situation.

Alex acknowledged with effusive admiration and glowing respect the president's strengths. But he spoke of the president's excesses with painful apology mixed with irritation, while eagerly admitting his own excesses. The note of apology was an ever-present theme with Alex. I had observed it before in meetings. I thought that made sense. It is part of the excess in Adapting-Dealing.

Gently, I indicated to Alex that I had frequently heard this note of apology in meetings, that it seemed it always followed or preceded a strong statement about his viewpoint on a problem. Alex paused, looked surprised, and went on to say that these feelings of apology were his plague. No matter what he did, he had feelings that it was never enough. And when he accomplished something outstanding, he had to make light of it.

According to Alex, his life had consisted of one series of achievements followed by public recognition and awards. That's the way he had geared his life—for accomplishment and recognition. From elementary school awards to college awards. From athletic awards to industry awards. But no awards from the president. Was it any wonder that he sent out that self-praising memo for a job well done? He would receive his award even if he had to bestow it on himself!

Alex revealed that this striving was encouraged by his mother who was from the "old country." The achievement and award sequence was her standard for living. She had wanted Alex to succeed in everything that he did. As soon as he had an award, she directed him to the next accomplishment. He felt that he could never please her. Not being able to please the president rekindled these feelings. The source of his dissatisfaction was in his own past experience and in the chance differences of his style and the president's.

With the workbook, Alex and I examined the catalytic effect the president and he might have on each other. We looked at the most effective and the least effective working situations for them both.

MOST EFFECTIVE SITUATIONS

THE PRESIDENT
Conserving-Holding

- Unemotional
- Factual
- Inquiring
- Practical

ALEX
Adapting-Dealing

- Exciting
- Social
- Accepting
- Flexible

LEAST EFFECTIVE SITUATIONS

THE PRESIDENT	*ALEX*
Conserving-Holding	Adapting-Dealing

- Constantly changing rules and policies
- Highly emotional
- Premature decision-making
- Failure to be taken seriously

- Firm schedules and supervision
- Critical authority
- Routines and details
- Formal and serious

What they clearly needed to do was to bridge and manage their differences. This did not seem so impossible because both had Controlling-Taking as their common ground to cross over to each other's world. So we looked in the workbook at "What's Best for Someone Who Is Conserving-Holding" like the president.

WHAT'S BEST FOR CONSERVING-HOLDING

To Influence and Motivate:

- Present ideas as low risk
- Give the opportunity to be analytical
- Exercise logic, use facts and structure
- Tie new things to old

To be the Most Effective Employee:

- Move ahead slowly
- Use logic
- Pay attention
- Be systematic
- Do your "homework"

After considering these guidelines, Alex and I discussed in what manner he had gone about investigating the pricing information. He had, in fact, done his homework, and although he was acting out of his least preferred orientation, Conserving-Holding, this was exactly how the president would prefer to see things accomplished. That was probably why the president was not as upset as Alex assumed when Alex sold the new product at the lower price.

Clearly, Alex had shown that he could use more Conserving-Holding strengths if he had to. It was possible to make a conscious effort to use them on other occasions. I explained that to fill in his blind spots, he did not have to change himself. He did not have to give up Adapting-Dealing or Controlling-Taking. He needed only to *add* some of the strengths and strategies of Conserving-Holding.

So that Alex would not feel the total responsibility for the bridging, we examined what the president could do in turn to work more effectively with Alex.

WHAT'S BEST FOR ADAPTING-DEALING

To Influence and Motivate:

- Give him or her the chance to do things with others
- Use humorous appeals
- Let it be known what pleases
- Provide him opportunities to be in the spotlight

To be the Most Effective Boss:

- Express intent and preference
- Be friendly and informal
- Give helpful feedback
- Provide the lay of the land
- Show flexibility
- Display a sense of humor

Three hours had passed quickly. Alex was feeling excited, relieved, and appreciative. Though these reactions were to be expected from the process we had just been through, Alex's enthusiasm and emotion were typical of his Adapting-Dealing orientation, but slightly in excess. While his enthusiasm could provide the energy for bridging, there would be some trial and error, some steps backward.

But he had a direction, new guidelines, and a new way of

looking at his relationship with the president. That was important because he decided to stay with the company. With bridging as a possiblity, the prospects for continued success were more promising. Alex could be more productive and more personally satisfied without the discouraging undertone in his key relationship with the president.

This crisis also had become an opportunity for Alex. It focused on his missing game plan, the blind spot caused by his least preferred orientation. Alex could now fill in his blind spot with total perspective for solving problems and making decisions. That meant less chance to be hit on his blind side by unforeseen events.

8

COMMUNICATION GAPS

THE FAULT OF THE GOLDEN RULE

The Golden Rule is a timeless moral precept, but it does not work well in communications. We are taught from childhood on, "Do unto others as you would have others do unto you." But not everybody is interested in the same things, not everybody wants to be treated the same way. They do not necessarily want to be treated the way *we* want to be treated.

We have to do unto others the way *they* want to be done unto. We have to approach them from the viewpoint of *their* game plan.

Actually, there are four Golden Rules, one for each orientation. Each orientation requires treatment consistent with its own game plan. If we learn to communicate in a way that matches these game plans, people will be more receptive, more tuned in to us.

Imagine yourself in front of your TV set. You're waiting for your favorite show to come on Channel 2. It's time for it to begin, but a different program is on the channel. You wait and wait, and you start getting irritated. When is it coming on? Finally you remember, it's on Channel 4! You switch over and become more relaxed as the program's familiar format unfolds.

Each orientation has its own familiar format, its own

FOUR COMMUNICATION CHANNELS

Information That Gets Through
to Each Orientation

SUPPORTING-GIVING

Channel 1

Wants Information on
Quality, Benefits to All,
and Relevancy.

CONTROLLING-TAKING

Channel 2

Wants Information on
Obstacles and Opportunities.
Who's in Charge?

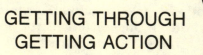

GETTING THROUGH
GETTING ACTION

CONSERVING-HOLDING

Channel 3

Wants Information on
How It Works,
Alternatives, and
Prior Performance.

ADAPTING-DEALING

Channel 4

Wants Information on
Acceptability and How
to Get Others to
Like It.

channel. Yet, we send our communications over *our* favorite channel, assuming other people are interested in the same things we are. It does no good to transmit a message on Channel 4 to someone who is watching on Channel 2. We need to communicate on each other's channels. And since there are four orientations, there are four channels, four ways to communicate. The diagram on page 76 illustrates this.

Because the four orientations to life each contain basic game plans, they give rise to four sets of basic life questions. These questions remain uppermost in our minds, regardless of the subject matter being presented to us. We stay "tuned in" if people answer these questions.

If these questions are not answered early in the communication, we generate tension and interference—static in the communication. That makes it difficult to get through to us. Answering these questions opens up the reception on our channel. These questions are basic, but crucial. They pervade our thinking in every area of our lives. They are listed below.

THE UPPERMOST QUESTIONS FOR EACH ORIENTATION

SUPPORTING-GIVING QUESTIONS

- How much good does it do, and for whom?
- Is it the best possible for all concerned?
- Does it have a high purpose?
- Is it fair and just?

CONTROLLING-TAKING QUESTIONS

- What are the opportunities?
- Who's in charge?
- What's the bottom line?
- How does it advance my position?

CONSERVING-HOLDING QUESTIONS

- How does it work?
- Where has it been done before?
- What alternatives are available?
- Can we try it a step at a time?

ADAPTING-DEALING QUESTIONS

- What are other people saying about it?
- How can we get others to like it?
- Can we change it if we don't like it?
- Will this bring us together more?

To open up channels of communication, those are the questions that need answering. That is the information each orientation requires. When we convey information that answers those questions, we are acknowledging the other person's orientation, who they are, and how they like to be treated.

The sooner the questions are answered, the sooner people give their attention. They also stay tuned in longer and give full consideration, because we are broadcasting on their channel.

Now, we are fortunate when our communication gets through easily to the other person, because they are like us and enjoy the same orientation. But since there are four orientations, the odds are three-to-one against our sending and receiving on the same channel. Three out of four times we could be sending on the wrong channel.

It is possible that in our family circle, or among our co-workers, we all share the same orientation. It does happen. More than likely, however, there are several key people in our lives who do not share our orientation.

This is where the trouble lies. This is where our tension mounts, as we sit and wait impatiently for our favorite programming from them, and it is not forthcoming because they are broadcasting over their own preferred channel. The problem in the relationship could be as simple as turning to the other person's channel. We may not realize the obvious, that we are just a turn of the dial away!

We spend time and energy insisting, "Impossible! There is no way to get through to this person. I've tried for years, and it can't be done." Yet how freeing it would be to discover that we are only tuned into the wrong channel! That we *can* reach those people who don't seem to be "on the same wavelength."

Think about some key people in your life who do not seem to be responding to your communications as well as you would like. What are their favorite orientations? Have you been answering their uppermost questions? Are you treating them the way *they* want to be treated, or are you treating them the way *you* want to be treated?

Don't be surprised if you discover that their most preferred orientation is your least preferred. That's the way it works all too often.

No wonder you don't enjoy communicating with them. You're at different ends of the dial! If you had liked *that* orientation, you would have had it for your first choice long ago. But you don't like it. In fact, how could anybody like it? Why is excellence so important to them, or action, or reason, or harmony? Who cares about their kinds of questions. They do.

What can be done if we are opposite? Well, for one thing, remember that we don't have to become like the people who are different from us to communicate with them. We don't have to change ourselves to improve our communication with key people in our lives. What is required is that we take a small amount of time to think, to anticipate their questions, and to answer them.

While the formula is simple, its execution calls for effort. It doesn't come naturally. We seem to expect the people with whom we work or live to make the effort toward us, to acknowledge our preferences first, do things and communicate the way *we* want. It would be so simple if only they were more like us—more idealistic, more take-charge, more systematic, or more tactful.

By organizing our communications to answer the uppermost questions of the key person, we provide ourselves with alternatives from our usual way of communicating with the person. It is a change of pace, a different sound and look that can capture attention, get interest, and stir action.

HOW TO ASK FOR A RAISE

For example, suppose you want to get a raise from your boss. You mention it in passing one day, but your boss doesn't respond. In fact, your comment seems to go unnoticed.

Finally you ask for a meeting to discuss it. Depending upon your own orientation, you will make an appeal to establish why you should get the raise.

The Boss's Game Plan Is Controlling-Taking

If your orientation is Supporting-Giving, you probably will explain how hard you worked, the long hours you put in, how much you need the raise. You might also state how fair it is in relation to what other people are making. But your boss's orientation could be Controlling-Taking and your appeal may not be heard. Therefore, it does not stir the boss.

If, on the other hand, you could turn to the boss's Controlling-Taking channel, you would emphasize different information consistent with what the boss needs to know. You could say something like, "Look, I don't want to pat myself on the back, but let me tell you what I accomplished over the last six months." You proceed to enumerate your *results,* your accomplishments. Then you say, "Let me tell you about my plans for the next six months. I've uncovered an exciting new opportunity. The bottom line is, it will definitely move us ahead. We'll be the first organization to offer the program. We'll have the jump on everybody."

Most likely, the boss would lean forward and hang on each word. The boss might think, "I better put that raise through, I don't want to dampen that desire. That's what I call hustle. That's getting things done."

The Boss's Game Plan Is Conserving-Holding

But suppose your orientation is Controlling-Taking and your boss is Conserving-Holding. As is characteristic of Controlling-Taking, you are filled with excitement and enthusiasm over your accomplishments, and you express it. You relate your accomplishments and your plans for the future, how you will seize opportunities to put your organization out in front, ahead of everybody else.

But your boss, whose orientation is Conserving-Holding,

may say, "All well and good, but what's so great about being first? 'Fools rush in where angels fear to tread.' And it will take more than raw enthusiasm to bring all that about. We need to take things a step at a time, see what happens, have some alternatives to fall back on. After we try out your new ideas and see how they affect what we've already got, then we'll talk about a raise."

Here's what would make more sense to this boss whose orientation is Conserving-Holding. You could say, "I did some homework and checked out salary ranges in comparable organizations. People in my position are making this kind of money. Here is the top, middle, and bottom of the range. Of course, position titles vary from organization to organization, so I made sure I was comparing truly like responsibilities.

"I'm just below the middle of the range. But before rushing into a decision, you need to consider whether my past accomplishments will hold up. Here's what I plan to do to make sure we get the most out of what we've got. I'm also watching for any negative impact. Here are some new ideas I want to try, but I won't go ahead until I have more history from the trial programs of other organizations."

The boss is probably saying, "That's my kind of person—deliberate, thinks things through, and doesn't go off the deep end. I don't want to take a chance on losing somebody like that, somebody who has their feet on the ground, somebody who really makes sense."

The Boss's Game Plan Is Supporting-Giving

Another possibility can be that you prefer Adapting-Dealing, but the boss is Supporting-Giving. You walk into the boss's office all smiles. The boss pushes aside a full in-basket of correspondence and reports to give you complete attention and concern. In your Adapting-Dealing way, you certainly don't want this to get too heavy, so you try to give it the light touch.

"If any more papers pile up on your desk, we'll have to start a salvage drive to help you get rid of them." The boss responds, "Let's be serious, we've got too much to do."

"Sure, I understand. Is there any way I can help you

reduce your workload?" After a brief interchange about how you can help, you feel the time is right to bring up the salary issue.

"You know, one way I could help is with the salary reviews. If you want me to go over them with you, I could give you my experience with the people. I know what they expect and that will satisfy them." You smile and add, "And while we're at it, I can give you my unbiased opinion of myself."

The boss squirms and replies, "It won't be necessary. I have my standards set already. I've developed an equitable plan and everybody will be treated fairly."

It seems like a closed case and there is no chance for discussion. But if you want to open the boss's mind, try communicating on the Supporting-Giving channel. You could emphasize the information that the boss needs to know. You could say, "All the people who work with me are putting out 110 percent. They're the hardest working group I've had the privilege to work with. I don't think you'll find more dedicated and loyal people. And I know it's immodest, but I include myself in those comments. We try harder, and the high standards we have maintained prove it. We've never cut corners to excel."

The boss might respond, "It's true, they seldom complain about the workload. They get the job done, and well. They don't give in to expediency when they're pushed. They just work harder. It's only fair that you all be rewarded for that kind of effort. And I like the way you admire and speak well of the group. You have a lot of character."

The Boss's Game Plan Is Adapting-Dealing

Bosses with Adapting-Dealing as their orientation need different information. Suppose you like Conserving-Holding, then your approach to getting a raise could sound like this. "Well, I've shaped up our projects and everything is in order. 'A place for everything, and everything, in its place,' I always say. You've got to have a system. We're really organized, all right, and we haven't gone in for any of those new programs which don't have a track record. Those could throw us off our plan. We've made the most of what we already have. There's been hardly any waste, and we've used up what we had on hand. Objectively speaking, I think our compensation plan should be proportional to what we've saved."

With the Adapting-Dealing orientation, this boss may be thinking by now, "I wonder if they saved string and paper clips, too? When's the last time they got out of their routine and tried something new? They're always so serious. They seem to be more concerned about their precious plans and systems than people."

To have this boss tune in, the Adapting-Dealing questions need to be answered. The approach could be, "Well, we've got our work in good shape. Our projects with other groups are running smoothly. We're so well organized that we haven't made one of our embarrassing mistakes in a long while. In fact, we've helped cut down on the confusion between our group and some of the others. We were flattered when some of them asked us to help install a similar system. As a result, there are virtually no more hassles between us. And another thing about our system that the other group likes is the time they save now. They'll be able to try out some new ideas and have more time to get together, to talk things out, to calm any troubled waters."

Responding more positively, the boss might say, "I'm glad they like it. There's nothing that wastes time like a needless argument. Life is too short. I'm glad things are smoothed over. You're a steady influence. Your organizational ability can keep us together. I'll see that the right people know about the system. We'll save a lot of time and money, and you'll share in the savings, if I have anything to say about it."

In these examples are some typical options for communicating on the other person's preferred channel. Notice that we don't have to change ourselves or become like the other person. Rather, we need only to *emphasize* the relevant information in our situation to match the other person's orientation.

In the table below, there are suggested approaches for communicating with each orientation. These strategies take into account the questions that are uppermost in the minds of people with that orientation. The recommendations suggest how to send your message on the other person's channel.

If the other person's most preferred orientation is . . .

Supporting Giving	Controlling Taking	Conserving Holding	Adapting Dealing
Try . . .	Try . . .	Try . . .	Try . . .
Indicating your need to be heard and stress the fairness and helpfulness of your idea.	Stating your point quickly and directly, with enthusiasm and confidence.	Presenting your point logically, in a well organized and factual manner.	Using a personable, light approach. Being fully informative as soon as possible.
Showing it is consistent with their principles and standards for excellence.	Indicating the challenges involved, and the opportunities for action and payoff.	Using the familiar, tying new things to old. Showing that your idea involves low risk.	Spending some socializing time before pressing for a decision. Showing flexibility and willingness to compromise.
Showing it is the right thing to do, good for all concerned, and the best possible solution.	Indicating the extent to which they will be in charge, and how they could miss an opportunity if they don't act now.	Documenting how the idea has worked in the past, has been checked out thoroughly, and that action is needed to preserve what they already have.	Showing that you have tested the waters, and that this action meets the approval of the majority of the people involved.

HOW TO PLAN A VACATION

Suppose you plan a vacation with a key person in your life. You want very much to go. In fact, you have been working hard and need the rest, but the other person is undecided, if not reluctant, to go. How would you try to influence the person? What would you say if their orientation was Supporting-Giving? Or Controlling-Taking? Or Conserving-Holding? Or Adapting-Dealing?

SUPPORTING-GIVING

Let's look at the approach to use if the person you're trying to influence prefers Supporting-Giving. The important points here are to emphasize your own needs, ask for help, show that what you want is consistent with their principles, and that it is the best possible way to do it.

Your communication might sound like this, "I've really been working hard lately, and I need a change. I think I'll be able to do more good when I get back. I don't want my work to suffer, and I certainly don't want to let anybody down. They depend on me.

"Here are a few travel folders. I'd like your help in deciding on a place that might be best for us. I've marked one that hasn't been spoiled by the tourists yet, and the staff apparently takes a real interest in the well-being of their clientele."

CONTROLLING-TAKING

On the other hand, if the person you are trying to convince is Controlling-Taking, the following approach is more meaningful. Be brief and direct, show your enthusiasm, state the opportunity for action, and state how they might be challenged. Let them have the first choice. You can say, "I know you don't have a great deal of time for planning our vacation, so I already went through a stack of travel folders. Here are the two most exciting places I found. There's a lot to do. We won't be bored, that's for sure.

"I don't think any of our friends have been there yet. Both places have several sports you've been dying to try. There's an off-season special for another month. We can beat the deadline. There's no time like the present. Which one of these two looks like the one for you?"

CONSERVING-HOLDING

But if the key person prefers Conserving-Holding, the emphasis is on tying new things to old, being factual, objective, organized, and showing that the plan is logical and low risk. Try this, "Remember our vacation last year, how much you liked the place? Well, I've uncovered two new places that are similar, but they also have some advantages over last year's. I had our travel agent give me a thorough rundown on the recreation facilities, the accommodations, the food, and the accessibility to transportation, so there won't be any unpleasant surprises. I've outlined the details from the travel agent and clipped them to the travel folders."

ADAPTING-DEALING

A key person who is Adapting-Dealing will respond to the following focus. Be definite about your opinion as soon as possible, indicate the potential for having fun, your willingness to be flexible, to compromise, and highlight the prestige and popularity of the places.

"I'm sold on this one place. It sounds like we'd have the most fun here. But I brought several other travel folders for you to look at because you might want to go to one of these—which will be fine with me. I'm looking forward to the trip, wherever we go.

"Several people at work have been to the resort I'm suggesting, and they say it's the 'in' place. Even though it's informal, they say a lot of well-known people stay there. It sounds like we'd meet new friends."

HOW TO COMMUNICATE TO CHILDREN

Now let's look at some applications of the Life Orientations Golden Rule ("Do unto others as they would have you do unto them.") in relationships between parents and children. For example, a typical problem with children is wanting to play, or watch TV, rather than do their homework.

SUPPORTING-GIVING

If, for instance, a child in the sixth grade favors Supporting-Giving, the parent's approach would be in this direction: "I know you want to watch TV, but I'm concerned for you and how it will affect your homework. You said that you wanted to keep up your good work at school, but if you watch any more TV today, will you be able to do your best? What you do today is important, because next semester the program gets harder. Everyone has to try harder to keep up. If you start your homework now, I'd like to review it with you later, to see if you have any questions."

CONTROLLING-TAKING

For a child whose main orientation is Controlling-Taking, a consistent communication for their orientation would unfold like this: "Say, I hear that the new program at school is getting harder. I hope it won't be too hard for you kids. But I know you like a challenge. If you want to get ahead in your generation, you have to keep up with changes. I'd like you to explain it to me. You can become more expert by teaching me about it. That's a faster way to learn. You can keep a step ahead. If you get out your homework, I'm not busy right now."

CONSERVING-HOLDING

A youngster who prefers a Conserving-Holding orientation responds to a message that emphasizes these points: "That new program really makes sense. It's so logical that it's harder to make mistakes. What I noticed was that you can learn it in steps. You don't have to do it all at once. It ties in with your work last year, too. I think that everything you're doing now will lay the groundwork for next year. If you get started with some of your homework now, you won't have to rush later. Then you'll have plenty of time to finish after supper. But in case you don't, you can tie up loose ends before breakfast."

ADAPTING-DEALING

When the child's preferred orientation is Adapting-Dealing, try this. "Your new school program really impresses me. I like it. I saw a teacher being interviewed on TV last night. The teacher was saying that many teachers and parents want to expand it into more schools next year. I understand that they may select some students to showcase the program. Maybe you would like to try out for it. Wouldn't it be something if you got on TV? Even if they don't go to that extent, the program is the coming thing. Most of your friends will be into it. It would please me to learn more about it. Why don't we review your homework together."

* * *

You could be saying to yourself at this point, "What do you think I am, a chameleon? How can I switch from one approach to another? I'm me. If somebody can't get my message the way it's natural for me, then we shouldn't be trying to communicate." That's an understandable reaction, but it won't help you get through to people. After reading the previous examples, perhaps you recognize that most of the orientations give you no trouble in communicating. Perhaps, though, one is emerging as a problem. That one doesn't seem understandable or workable to you. If you can't figure out why anybody would want to live their life like that, if you feel uncomfortable even using the words in that approach, I'll wager that is *your* least preferred orientation.

If that is your reaction, it is a frequent one. It means that when you try to work with, or live with, or just communicate with people who prefer that orientation as their main choice, you will inevitably confront difficulty. But if you can learn to appreciate their orientation, let them supplement your own thinking, you can enhance your life considerably.

Ironically, the people who are different from you can share an entirely new perspective, open up new areas of thinking that can be of major value to you. They can supplement your life, your planning, and decision making. People who are oriented differently can add a perspective to fill in your blindspots, and help you avoid major mistakes and see opportunities that have been out of your line of vision. These people provide a check and balance for your excess—if you can appreciate their differences and use those differences positively, rather than allowing them to divide you.

To summarize, treating others the way that comes naturally to us may be ineffective in trying to get through and get action from them. We can't "do unto others" as we would have "others do unto us." We have to treat them the way *they* want to be treated. Because there are four orientations, four ways people like to be treated, there are four Golden Rules. Each orientation has its special approaches that get through, get acceptance, and get action.

If you're feeling frustrated with some key person in your life, try out some of these alternate approaches. They will give you a fresh point of view and a feeling that you're not doing the same old thing and getting the same old response. When you feel you are at an impasse, new options can give you a feeling of greater optimism and personal power.

To help you find alternate approaches more easily, here is a summary of suggested approaches to get through to the key people in your life.

HOW TO GET THROUGH TO KEY PEOPLE

APPROACHES TO SUPPORTING-GIVING

- Appeal to principles
- Emphasize self-development
- Ask for help
- Show concern
- Appeal to excellence

APPROACHES TO CONTROLLING-TAKING

- Emphasize action
- Offer opportunity
- Acknowledge initiative
- Spar on an equal basis
- Provide challenge

APPROACHES TO CONSERVING-HOLDING

- Be analytical and systematic
- Tie new things to old
- Use logic and structure
- Present ideas as low risk
- Be organized and prepared

APPROACHES FOR ADAPTING-DEALING

- Express your own preference
- Be friendly and informal
- Show flexibility
- Display sense of humor
- Indicate your approval

9

THAT'S NOT MY GAME

SO WHAT HAVE I GOT TO LOSE?

Plenty. More than you may realize. It can create a blind spot.

Traditionally, the term *blind spot* has meant that one's thoughts, feelings, or ideas have been repressed. They have been pushed out of awareness, their existence denied. It has meant something that is unacceptable to our conscious self, something that has gone underground.

Blind spot, in Life Orientations Theory, means an angle of view that is cut off from our vision. On the right side of a car, for example, between the rear window and the side window, the body of the car creates a blind spot. When we look over our shoulder to see if anyone is coming up alongside, we do not have total information, and if it is a small car, coming alongside, we may miss it entirely.

So it is with our vision of life situations—there is a piece out of our view. And it is our least preferred orientation that is out of our view, creating a blind spot, interrupting us from a total 360-degree perspective.

Look at your least preferred orientation. These are questions you need to ask to get a total perspective on what you're doing.

Usually, we pay very little attention to our least preferred orientation, or to the people who follow that game plan. In

In the diagram below, see if you can identify your blind spot.

The 360° Viewpoint for Total Perspective

What information are you missing?

SUPPORTING-GIVING

• I provide:

Information on quality.
Benefits to all, and
relevancy.

• I ask:

How much good does it do?
And for whom?

CONTROLLING-TAKING

• I provide:

Information on opportunities
and obstacles.

• I ask:

Who is in charge?
What is the advantage to us?

**PLANS
GOALS
PROBLEMS
DECISIONS
RELATIONSHIPS**

ADAPTING-DEALING

• I provide:

Information on acceptability
and on how to get others to
like it.

• I ask:

How do you pull together
differences into a harmonious
whole?

CONSERVING-HOLDING

• I provide:

Information on alternatives,
steps and procedures.

• I ask:

How does it work?
Where has it been done
before?

fact, those people may appear so foreign to us that we avoid them. They are not our kind, someone on our own wavelength.

However, if we are forced by circumstances, or if we are attracted to them for other reasons, we can become frustrated in trying to get along. We like them, admire them, love them, but we just can't "see" why they do things the way they do. If we don't allow their differences in viewpoint to supplement us, our view of problems and solutions is incomplete.

To cover all the bases and to protect ourselves when making big plans and big decisions, we need only to go through the thinking process of each orientation by asking ourselves the questions germaine to each. But we can go one step further. We can *extend* our strengths by learning to act more comfortably with the strengths of our least preferred orientation.

Over time, this would mean that some of the strengths of our *least* preferred orientation would become second nature to us. We would not have to think twice about using them, or about relating to someone who preferred that orientation most.

Surprisingly, it could be an area of growth, offering us extended options. Let me explain what I mean by using my own experience as an example.

In the early days of developing Life Orientations Theory and Training, it was difficult for me to understand or appreciate Conserving-Holding. My preferred game plans were primarily Controlling-Taking and Adapting-Dealing. The results of the Life Orientations Survey showed how little Conserving-Holding fit into my way of doing things. I was traveling around the country, going from one program to another, and enjoying the pace and variety. It was difficult for me to take one thing at a time and consolidate my effort in an organized way.

When I would give a presentation on the four orientations, I discovered that I talked about the Controlling-Taking way with great facility and ease, even enthusiasm. Adapting-Dealing, which as my second choice, was also easy for me to describe, and the clarity of my understanding was communicated. Supporting-Giving was a bit more difficult, and my explanations and descriptions were less thorough.

Finally, when I had to describe Conserving-Holding, I felt quite mechanical and intellectual about it. I was describing it from the outside in, rather than the inside out. I could get my mind around it, but I couldn't get my heart into it.

Even more difficult for me was working with people whose game plan was Conserving-Holding. I found myself uncomfortable, ill at ease, and sometimes even frustrated with them. It was doubly difficult for me because as a professional and creator of Life Orientations Training, I felt I "ought" to be able to understand all the orientations. My theory said there was no one best game plan and that all plans were valid. Reconciling this difference between my theory and personal reaction was important. I like to practice what I "preach."

"What's going on?" I asked myself. "Why do I feel so remote and distant to this particular orientation? Who could have influenced me? Why did I seldom look out of this window to the world? Why was I so unaccustomed to it?" Some vague recollections began to emerge.

Was it possible? Yes, during the Depression in the 1930's, while I was growing up, we had very little money. My mother could really make do, make the most of what we had. With our old furniture, she would make new arrangements in the living room. Other rooms would look completely different. She would change slip covers and add a few pillows. It was the same old stuff, but it always looked new.

Ah, but on the other hand, I remembered, she always needed to know where I was, what I was doing. I had to report. She'd inquire, "Where'd you go? Who'd you see? What'd you do?" She needed her certainty, her predictability—even in later years when she visited me in California. Her plane would arrive, and we'd exchange hugs and kisses, get the baggage, and drive off in the car. Immediately, she'd ask, "What are we going to do tomorrow? I'd like to see Aunt Janet on Thursday. Friday we can go to a Studio, and Saturday I want to go to Disneyland. When we get to the house, let's call the airline and reconfirm my reservation back to Philadelphia."

I experienced my mother's Conserving-Holding as an excess, as indeed it was at times—her need to know, to be sure, seemed investigative. I began to actively reject that way of doing things, even though there were the obvious strengths of making the most of what we had. The excess was annoying, and I decided not to favor Conserving-Holding.

Now, years later, I wondered if I could learn more about Conserving-Holding, learn how other people make it work, to see if I could increase my appreciation of it, and perhaps even use more Conserving-Holding strengths in my own life.

I thought about a consulting assignment in which all the key executives preferred Conserving-Holding as their first or second choice. I remembered how dismayed I was to learn this. They were so matter-of-fact in meetings. The atmosphere was cool and objective. They could calmly discuss potentially volatile issues, or people-problems, and even their successes and failures. Yet, their way of handling things seemed so foreign to me. I found myself wondering, "Don't these people get excited or annoyed about anything? Must everything be handled so mechanically? How do they discuss things when they need to clear the air?"

Fortunately for me, the colleague with whom I was working preferred the Conserving-Holding orientation, as well as Controlling-Taking. Through him, my exposure to this group taught me that clearing the air can come through the thoroughness of everyone's thinking, not necessarily a confrontation or heated debate. Getting outwardly enthusiastic was less important to them than the satisfaction of covering all the ramifications of an issue. I could see the benefits of more patience, thoroughness, and structure. He was the perfect supplement to this consulting experience.

After watching my colleague in action, I began to practice some Conserving-Holding strengths and made a deliberate effort to add them to my life and work. For example, on three-by-five cards, I wrote key phrases. One said, "Think now, act later," another, "Take a second look." Another said, "Opportunity knocks twice." A final card read, "You don't have to respond immediately—it won't go away."

Beside my desk near the telephone, I taped them on the wall as constant reminders. When a call came from a client, and I was asked to do a project, instead of responding immediately, I'd say, "Well, I need to talk this over with the staff," or, "Let me think more about it and call you back tomorrow." My surprise was that most clients did not mind being put off for awhile—if they thought their questions would be more thoroughly analyzed.

I learned to explore alternatives, to be more thorough and systematic. It felt like a grind at first. I thought I was plodding. I experienced the strengths as if I were using them excessively. But with my need for action there was no fear of getting stuck on dead center, or slowing down into analysis paralysis. It took a year, but I learned to extend myself, and to add a new game plan and some new strengths.

Remember, extending our strengths from our least preferred orientation is an option. We can go through life with few major mistakes and lost opportunities if we are fortunate enough to be supplemented by people who are different from us. But the supplementing people may not always be available. It is extra insurance if we can eliminate our own blind spots and achieve total perspective.

When we make major mistakes, they often center around common errors. Errors come from an incomplete view of reality, resulting from our least preferred orientation. We will be missing the answers to the important questions that arise from that orientation, answers that contribute to the picture of total reality. Without answering all of the questions generated by the four orientations, we have only partial information with which to solve our problems and make important decisions.

ERRORS AND LOST OPPORTUNITIES

Here are some common errors to which we are vulnerable, depending on our *least* preferred game plan.

Too Little Supporting-Giving

When our least preferred is Supporting-Giving, we could overlook issues of fairness and whether people were being justly treated. Unfairness or injustice could take place around you without your noticing it or reacting to it.

Some people could consider you indifferent to activity which had a high or idealistic purpose. You could have difficulty in influencing people who are concerned about excellence as an end goal, and you could accept minimum quality that could create problems later on. You could also be vulnerable to making decisions for today that didn't plan far enough into the future for all concerned.

Too Little Controlling-Taking

Possible errors are different if our least preferred orientation is Controlling-Taking. Frequently, what we will overlook is the advantage in certain plans, an advantage that could advance our position. Others more often will see the opportunity to advance their position and will seize it, leaving us in the same circumstances, watching others move quickly.

Being in command will not be important. Seeing opportunities for it will go unnoticed. Others will more frequently be in charge of situations, appearing to dominate them. Sometimes, too, we may be so immersed in one activity that we lose sight of the end results and overlook the need for quick action to head off a problem or a crisis.

Too Little Conserving-Holding

Conserving-Holding presents some other possibilities for error when it is preferred least. A common one is reinventing the wheel, wasting time and money doing something from scratch that was done before. Usually, there was no effort to check it out beforehand. We can also overlook the effect of dropping something old for something new, and we may miss the utility and practical value still left in the old way. Unknowingly, we may waste time and money in our effort to do something new, or better, or something that is more pleasing.

Often, without paying enough attention to Conserving-Holding we will overlook the mechanics that make it difficult for things to work out. Laborious little things and troublesome inconsistencies will be overlooked, and we will say, "Don't bother me with details." When something goes wrong, though, it is difficult to see our own contribution. It all looked so easy to us when we "skimmed across the water seeing only the tips of icebergs."

Without sufficient Conserving-Holding perspective, it is very likely that we will jump into a thing with both feet, rather than taking it a step at a time. We will act now and think later, and we will go back and correct our omissions rather than anticipate them through a trial run with a manageable sample.

Too Little Adapting-Dealing

The possible major errors from under-utilizing the Adapting-Dealing game plan are around flexibility, compromise, and empathy. Without the aid of this orientation, we are likely to stand up so strongly for what we believe and what we want that we miss the areas of compromise.

Others may experience us as unshakable or unbendable. We may get our wants filled, but may cause a serious break in a relationship as the price. The message to others will be that we value the accomplishment more than the relationship. With this blind spot, we may wonder why others suddenly removed themselves from the relationship, became competitive, or became an adversary.

We may have the best ideas, but we will find it difficult to get others to implement them. Our ideas will sometimes fall short in execution because people will not get behind them. Probably you will overlook the time needed to involve the doers by early participation in the planning.

Without Adapting-Dealing, we may have the best of intentions to help people, but we will be way off the mark because we are not in tune with their needs and wants. Instead, we will offer help in a way that would be meaningful to us, not them. We will not place ourselves in their shoes, to get the "feel" of them.

For most of us, we usually overlook at least one orientation. That's how we try to simplify our lives—making choices by eliminating alternatives. But when it comes to orienting ourselves when making major decisions, planning for the future, or presenting important proposals, we had better take a 360-degree look from the viewpoint of all four orientations.

We need the information that each can provide for *total perspective* and *total power*. No one's judgment and effectiveness is better than the completeness and accuracy of their information. Each orientation makes its own unique contribution toward that end.

10

THE CASE OF THE
BLACK GODFATHER
AND THE BLAME GAME

"A palace revolution is about to take place." Jack Phillips, the executive vice-president, was joking, but there was a note of alarm beneath his humor.

He laughed, "It may not be that bad, but things have gotten out of hand in administration for the past three months. The head of administration and one of his managers are at war with another manager. It's the boss and purchasing against data processing."

I wondered why Jack had waited so long to call me. I voiced some concern, "The longer tensions build, the tougher they are to turn around."

"Well," Jack responded, "I talked with the three of them, and the Vice President of Personnel did, too. All three had worked so well over the past four years, we thought a few meetings would clear it up. There's an armed truce at the moment, but they're all making accusations behind each other's backs. What do you say, Doc? Can you help on this one?"

"I'll see, Jack, but I need more information."

"Come to my office tomorrow afternoon. I'll juggle some appointments," Jack said with relief.

The following day, I settled into the soft leather chair in Jack's office. I felt myself mobilizing my attention. Managing

98

conflict is complex. It requires concentration and energy.

Jack cleared his desk, then his throat to prepare for his presentation. "They're troublesome, he said, shaking his head. "But all three are respected throughout the company. They're accomplished people."

Jack leaned forward in his chair. He began to tell me the story. When he had finished, I knew I had an explosive situation on my hands. It could have legal complications if the tensions were not put to rest.

Here's Jack's rundown. The boss, Sam Franklin, the head of administration, is an old-timer, sixty-four, and near retirement. Sam is from a wealthy family and doesn't need to work.

Sam is upset with his young black assistant, Elliot Hayes, who is in charge of data processing. Sam has brought Elliot along in the company the last four years, and they had worked harmoniously on key company projects. Suddenly, according to Sam's report, Elliot began running wild, being insubordinate, and creating trouble with the black workers in Nancy Parker's purchasing department.

Though Elliot has no authority over Nancy's people, he has been meeting with her black workers. He has lunch with them, invites them to his home, and regularly calls them into his office. Nancy feels that he is undermining her authority.

Nancy Parker has been with the company for twenty years, since she graduated from high school, starting in a clerical position and growing into a key management post. She has voiced her resentment to Sam about Elliot's crossing boundaries into her department.

When she has a problem with a black worker, Elliot winds up talking with that person about the problem. Nancy says that his intrusion is creating dissension, and it is causing a serious minority problem.

What's more, Nancy says that everyone in her department is aware of the tension between them, and people seem to be taking sides. The workers are more interested in the drama of Elliot and Nancy than in the work at hand.

Jack's description of the "palace revolution" concluded with the accusations and the cross-complaints of Sam, Elliot and Nancy.

While Nancy accuses Elliot of being militant and a troublemaker to serve his own ego, Elliot accuses Nancy of racial bias and of dumping her marital unhappiness on her workers.

Elliot also accuses the boss, Sam, of "retiring in place," just waiting out his time and filling it by being interested in all the young girls in his department.

Sam accuses Elliot of turning into a playboy, taking long lunches with people outside his department, ingratiating himself with anybody and everybody to feather his own nest.

As the executive vice president finished his rundown, he repeated his hope that he would not lose any of the three. But word was out that Elliot was already looking for a new job.

Though I had reservations, I felt that I had no choice in the matter. I had to take the assignment. The problem made the company too vulnerable for me to pass on this one.

"OK, Jack," I agreed. "This is a tough one, but I'll see what I can do."

In positioning me with Sam, Jack said that Sam was the final authority. Jack told Sam that my objective was twofold—salvage Elliot so that the company wouldn't lose an important asset, and solve Nancy's resentment so that she wouldn't leave either.

My plan was simply to hear Sam's version of the problem, Nancy's next, and then to interview Elliot. From these interviews, I would come up with my own version of what was going on, and proceed to reduce tensions.

Two days later, when I walked into Sam's office, I could feel a solemn air, a heaviness. He closed the door behind me. I was in it, now.

Sam was tall and thin. His light green shirt was rolled up at the sleeves. His movements were quick, sharp. He lit a cigarette. He leaned back in his swivel chair, and he asked me how much I knew about what was happening. I said that Jack had filled me in, generally, but that I would like to get the specifics directly from him—and how he felt about the situation.

"Well, the main thing to tell you is about Elliot. It's just a shame. Elliot has turned into a prima donna. I spent three years training him. We used to work so well together. We were a great one-two punch at top level meetings. We really complemented each other. But lately he's gotten impossible. His ego's out of hand. He takes these long, two-martini lunches with Nancy's people. He goes behind closed doors with them. He's stirring up trouble. He's become a chaplain, a Godfather to all her black workers."

Sam seemed personally disappointed in Elliot, not just boss to employee, but as if his son had gone wrong. The student was disappointing the mentor.

"If I ask him to do things in a hurry for me, I get them when he's damn well ready to give them to me. He's trying to run Nancy's people, and he should have nothing to do with Nancy or her people. He's even trying to boss some of my administrative staff. He's not supposed to act as second in command to our department. He has his own group to manage . . . You know, he's trying to steal the hearts and minds of my people!"

Sam's frustration and anger peaked. "I just can't contain him. He's into everything." Sam paused. I waited. "You know," he went on, "this all started about six months ago. The president reorganized some of my functions. He took three of my people and transferred them over to the controller's office. I think Elliot saw this as a sign that I was losing favor. Elliot misread the trail signs that I was on the decline, and he saw this as a chance for him to gain some power."

I knew that Sam had not lost favor, and I knew that the reorganization was for efficiency.

Sam lit another cigarette and his mood changed. He seemed to be weighing things in his mind. "You know," He reflected, "part of our problem is space. Elliot shouldn't even be in this building with me. If his group wasn't in the same building with Nancy's, he wouldn't be bumping into her people. That just encourages him. But there's nothing we can do about that at the moment."

"It looks like your rising star has turned into a falling comet," I commented.

"That's about it," Sam agreed, "and if this wasn't enough, Elliot's been pressing me about his title. He wants to be promoted from a manager to the director level. I've tried, but top management won't buy it. And for myself, I've been trying to get them to give me more responsibility. Hell, I can do my job with one hand tied behind my back. It's routine.

"Frankly, I don't need this job. I don't need the money. But I need to work in another sense. I've learned too much over the years, I just can't turn it off. I like business. I've saved the company a hell of a lot of money over the past seven years.

And I like people. I like to teach them. That's why I've got to work.

"Here, take a look at this picture—our Christmas party last year. See this young girl? Her name is Frances. She was going to be fired because of a drug problem. I hated to see that. She's so damn smart. I took her under my wing. She's been almost like a daughter to my wife and me. We made her one of the family, and she's doing just great.

"You see, I need to be in the thick of it, solving problems and bringing people along. But I don't have to be bored by routine, and I don't have to tolerate a good apple like Elliot turning rotten.

"I'm at my wit's end with him. See what you can do. I'd appreciate it." Sam stood up. I followed him to the door. He walked me downstairs to Nancy's office. She was behind her desk, waiting.

Nancy's posture was erect—not tense, but proper. She was wearing a gray gaberdine suit, and a yellow rose was pinned to her lapel. She looked young, but her seriousness veiled her youth. After pleasant introductions, Sam left.

Nancy asked me how we were going to proceed, how much time we needed, and what we hoped to accomplish together. I answered briefly, indicating that we would have an informal meeting of about one to one-and-a-half hours, in which she would tell me about the tensions going on. Then I said that I would interview Elliot and try to find ways to restore some calm in the situation.

She smiled and said, "I hope so. It would be wonderful to stop all this bickering and bad feeling. I'd like things back to normal. There's nothing but one surprise after another. You just can't predict what Elliot will do next. I really dislike being adversaries, but if that's the way he wants it, so be it."

She was resentful, but the resentment was cool, under control. As our discussion evolved, she continued in a matter-of-fact tone. "Look, the truth of the matter is, Elliot's on an ego trip. He's actually said to my face, 'You're running your deparment with favorites, and you're too hard on the others.' He implied that he knows how to run my department better than I do.

"He claims that I'm very subjective and let my feelings rule my good judgment. Nothing could be further from the truth. Besides, how I run my department is none of his business. I know I'm good. Do you know the volume of orders that we process here, and the dollars involved? Let me tell you that my department is a model in the industry.

"I get calls all the time from people wanting me to come to work for their company. It's flattering, but I've grown up here, so to speak. It's here I want to stay. But Elliot is making things so uncomfortable, those offers are sounding very good. I wish he had as much respect for me as they do. You know, I think he's very chauvinistic. He doesn't think a woman can run a department."

She paused and became reflective. "I just thought, you know, Elliot reminds me of my husband. He's on the run just like Elliot—a bundle of energy. And he's a male chauvinist, too. When I first got promoted to a supervisory job, he made a rule. No talking business at home. At home he wants me to be an oldfashioned wife, although he does help with the housework. But no business problems—I can't share any problems whatsoever. I've got two chauvinists, one at home and one at work. How lucky can you be."

Nancy seemed to be expressing the role of the victim, but her expression was cool and unemotional, just reporting the facts. Her hurt no doubt was concealed and reserved for other places.

Nancy looked out the window. I broke her reverie. "I understand that things used to be different, that all this trouble with Elliot is recent."

She thought for a minute. "As a matter of fact, it started about six months ago. Just after I promoted Susan as my assistant. To tell you the truth, that was my first mistake. I really wanted Cindy as my assistant. But Sam and Elliot were for Susan. They said Susan was better with people, even though she didn't have the experience in buying that Cindy had. Really, Cindy is smart as a whip. But, I went with the boss and Elliot, and now I'm sorry. Susan didn't catch on. She's conscientious, but she didn't understand our purchasing systems like Cindy did. I worked with Susan—gave her all the help I could—but she still didn't understand our systems. I suggested she take some courses, and her feelings were hurt.

"That's when Elliot got in the picture. He jumped to her rescue. Susan claimed I was being critical because she was black. But she really didn't have it, and I was stuck.

"Elliot started to have meetings with my people behind

closed doors. That's unnerving. The whole thing undercut my authority. If they had a problem, they would run to him. He's become the Godfather to all my black employees.

"I just don't understand what got into him. We can't go on this way. There's enough pressure with our purchasing load. It's doubled. I can't afford to put my time into this nonsense. We've all got too much to do. I've decided to reorganize my department and take over some of Susan's responsibilities."

I could feel Nancy's frustration, and I could see her bewilderment about Elliot's actions. It seemed that she needed to make sense out of the situation, as well as have it corrected. Nancy probably could not tolerate not knowing, and being out of control. In her office, she had a place for everything and everything was in its place.

As I left Nancy's office, I felt saturated with assumptions, facts, opinions and judgments which had been laid out by both Nancy and Sam. What was objective and what was subjective? I would have to sort it all out after seeing Elliot.

But Elliot was the target person, the object of the blame game. "If it only weren't for Elliot . . . " While I knew he could be a major contributor to the problem it was not likely that he was the sole source of the trouble. Sam and Nancy had to be contributors in the triangle.

The next day, I came back to see Elliot. As I walked through a narrow reception office, I could see a young man behind a desk in the inner office. He appeared busy but aware that I was approaching.

"Elliot?" I questioned. He stood up, smiled, and extended his hand. He was short and trim, aristocratic looking. His dress was dapper—a brown pin-striped suit with a vest. On the outside he seemed relaxed, but the eyes behind the goldrimmed glasses studied me carefully. It was that moment when two strangers meet. Behind his cordiality, I could feel his reserve.

For a brief time, we exchanged pleasantries. It was difficult to think about him as the menace portrayed by Nancy and Sam.

"Where do you want to start?" he asked.

"Just jump in anywhere. However you see things."

"That's fine with me. Well, this entire situation is ridiculous. It's simply got out of hand. Sam and Nancy are acting like kids. They're doing things that don't make sense. I just think their sins are catching up with them. Nancy is afraid of change, anything that upsets well-ordered routines. I've no patience with people who are afraid to change.

"Nancy's been managing the same way for fifteen years. In my field, if I didn't change, if I wasn't flexible, well, I'd be out. And speaking of change, I'll give it to you straight. If this situation doesn't change, I'm off to another company. I've got some good offers. I don't want to do that, but I will if I have to. I like it here. People like my work, and I like the people. I can still learn a lot from Sam, and I can still do a lot of good for this company.

"And believe it or not, despite the way Sam is acting lately, I enjoy working with him. He's been good to me. He gave me a chance to learn, to show what I can do. But he has some old-fashioned ways. If a woman cries, he gets nervous and wants to make things all right, instantly.

"That's what Nancy's done. She's got him wrapped around her little finger. He'll take the side of women every time. I've seen it. When Nancy complains about me, automatically I'm guilty in Sam's eyes. That's not fair to me. He treats me like a kid. I'm a big boy now. The company knows what I can do, and every department head works well with me. My work is outstanding. And I can even make it better."

As I listened, I thought Elliot was protesting against his old role with Sam. Elliot seemed to be saying that he did not want Sam to be his mentor anymore. He wanted recognition on his own, not just as part of the Sam-Elliot team.

Elliot expanded on this. "You know, he treats Nancy like his daughter. And me, he treats me like a son. He treats everybody that way, like his kids. He's very paternalistic. That's no way to manage.

"Nancy is just as bad. She's got her favorite, Cindy. She'd like Cindy to replace her assistant, Susan. Frankly, I don't think Nancy can work with Susan because she's black. I think we may have a racial problem here. Nothing Susan does pleases Nancy, and Susan's a capable girl. She's very good with people."

I interrupted Elliot. "I'm not so sure that's the case with Nancy. My impressions are that she really tries to be objective, and she truly thinks that Cindy is better qualified technically."

"Well, why in the hell did she promote Susan into that job in the first place? As the 'token black'?"

"No, I don't think so, Elliot. She promoted Susan because she thought it was important to you and Sam. She felt outvoted. You and Sam were a strong influence."

"But I'm not her boss. I've nothing to do with her department."

"Nevertheless, she sees you as acting like Sam's right-hand man, his second in command. You carry out some of his work. You give assignments to some of Sam's other people. Nancy and her employees apparently see you as trying to be boss."

"Well, that's crazy. I'm not trying to be boss. I'm just doing Sam's dirty work. He keeps giving me more and more things to do—the things he's bored with. I'm more than glad to help him out, but I'm damned if I'm trying to take over. I like my own work too much. It can keep me busy for a lifetime. It's more fun."

Elliot looked serious. "This is some joke. I'm damned if I do and damned if I don't. If I didn't help out Sam, then he'd say I was uncooperative. When I do help him out, they accuse me of trying to take over. If Sam's bored with his job, why doesn't he make top management give him more of a challenge? I don't know, maybe I should mind my own business. But I'll tell you this for sure, when he asks for help, I don't give it a second thought."

Elliot's frown reflected his double bind. He stood up and removed his coat, placing it over the back of the chair. As he sat down, he continued.

"It's the same thing with Nancy's people. It's none of my business, but when they come to me with a problem, I can't turn them down. I really tried to get them going in the right direction. I'd say, 'Talk it over with Nancy,' and they'd say, 'No use. She's got a closed mind.' Then I'd take them into my office and give them a good talking to. I've said to some of them, 'Look, you better shape up, try to get along, or your ass will be kicked out of here.'

"That may sound tough, but I care about them. I've made it, and I want them to make it, too. In fact, I feel responsible for them. So when they come to me, what am I supposed to do, tell them to go away? I can't turn my back on them."

Elliot was intense, pained by the dilemma of personal

caring and departmental boundaries. "Elliot, I know you can't turn your back on them. But it does diffuse Nancy's authority. And it lessens the possibility that they'll take their complaints to her directly—where something can be done about them. What's more, I believe Nancy would try. Though she might have a favorite, she does try to be objective."

"Well, I don't know." Elliot was skeptical. "I wish I could be as sure as you are."

"I feel very sure, Elliot. She cares about those people as much as you do, only she comes off as calm, cool and collected. That's the only difference between you."

Elliot listened intently. He thought to himself and nodded his head decisively. "OK. Here's what I'm going to do. When any of her people come to me, I'll send them right back to her. I'll just tell them I don't want anything to do with it."

"Elliot, I'm picking up a tone of 'to hell with it.' Like you're not appreciated for trying to help. Helping is not the trouble. It's the quantity, not the quality."

I hoped he caught the distinction. I wasn't commenting on the strength, just the excess.

"What I mean, Elliot, is they need to face Nancy directly. They won't as long as they have you. It's a lot easier to blow off steam with you, than to face their own boss with a problem. But that doesn't solve it. It only puts you and Nancy against each other."

Elliot forced his heels into the red rug and pushed his swivel chair back, placing more distance between us. I went on, "Her employees seem to be acting like kids, playing one parent against the other. If they don't like what mother's doing, they'll go to father. And it doesn't mean a damn thing if they're black or white or brown. That's just how kids are. And Nancy feels undercut because they're running to you. You're the big daddy."

"My God, are you telling me I'm paternal too, like Sam?"

"That's what seems to be going on."

"Wow, that astonishes me."

"I can see that."

"Well, I hope you set Nancy and Sam straight, because this situation isn't only my fault. Nancy has some problems."

"I'm sure she does. And she is working on them. But it's nobody's fault. Everybody contributes to the problem in their own unique way. I'm trying to sort out who is contributing to the problem in what way—then come up with some solutions."

Elliot was considering my statement. He seemed less intense. I continued, "I have a suggestion for you, and a caution. When the black employees come to you, watch your tone. It's important that you convey that you still care, that you're not suddenly dropping your interest in them. On the contrary, you need to convey that you think it's in their best interest to try to work out their problems with Nancy directly. You can be sympathetic, but you have to tell them that you have no influence in the situation. That you're not second in command."

"Second in command?" Elliot was surprised. "I've never told them I'm second in command. I'm not their boss."

"You know that, but apparently they see you as the boss."

"Sam and I do a lot of things together, but I'm not his second in command. There is no second in command."

"Well, they think you are. And I think it's Sam's impression that *you* think you are."

"Now wait a minute. This is crazy. I wouldn't be second in command of adminstration if you forced me. That's not what I want for my career. I'm a specialist. Data processing is my thing, and that's that. How in the hell did this second in command trip get laid on me?"

"I think I know."

"Well, enlighten me—fast, please," Elliot implored.

"I think it starts with your sense of responsibility. Your desire to be helpful and responsive to people."

"What are you telling me?"

"Well, Elliot, look. When someone comes to you with a problem, you want to respond, take care of it. You're quick, bright, caring. That's a combination that gets you involved. Department heads come to you for information, you help them get what they want. Sam comes to you for relief from some of his boring responsibilities, you help. Black employees come to you, you help."

Elliot was concentrating and carefully trying to follow my explanation. "Somebody has a need, a problem, you're in the middle of it. You're just being responsible and responsive. It looks like you want power, and you do. But it's power over problems, not people."

Elliot stared at me. He had that look of astonishment when somebody describes what's going on with you. "But, Elliot, you're taking on everybody's problems—to an excess. It's beginning to backfire. You're doing too much of a good thing."

"Too much of a good thing? There's nothing better than solving a problem. I thrive on it. And I must admit, I've had the opportunity here to do it. Sam's encouraged me. Nobody's stood in my way. My pay reflects my progress, too. And I've got more to learn and more problems to solve."

Elliot rolled his chair to the window. He looked out, and then turned back to me. "I've paid my dues, believe me. And I deserve something for it. I want to be on the Director level. I want to be on a more equal footing with the people I serve in the company. I want the department heads to know that the company recognizes my worth. It appreciates my work. Is that too much to ask?"

"I understand, Elliot. That's important to you."

"But don't misunderstand me about Sam. I still want to work with him. I can learn a lot more from him. But if I can't get the recognition here, I have several offers where I can. Now that's not a threat, it's just a fact."

I thought I heard an undertone of intimidation.

Elliot said with concern, "I hope I don't sound disloyal to Sam. If I wanted to be disloyal, I've had my chances. I never once said anything about Sam to the other department heads. I've always backed him up. You can check with any of them. I never undercut him—once."

"Elliot, that would be important for Sam to know. Have you ever told him that, and how much you've enjoyed working with him?"

"He must know it."

"Don't be too sure," I countered. "Being personal means a lot to Sam. He likes to be liked. My guess is that he's not feeling that you like him at this point."

"Look, I do my job and let the work speak for itself. Why can't he do the same? Why can't he see the ways I appreciate him by what I do in the department?"

"Well, for one thing, it was different when you started here. Then he had you under his wing. It was easy for him to feel appreciated, watching you soak up his advice. Now that you're flying around on your own, he doesn't feel needed. In

109

fact, he feels he's lost all control over you. You even want to leave the nest.''

"Well, I'm just not going to let this whole thing get to me. If he feels that way, that's his problem. I don't want to be unsympathetic, but I'm not going to get involved.''

"So you're going to let him hang there, by himself, even though he wants to make an impact on you?''

"I'll tell you this. He can't make an impact on me by criticizing who I lunch with and how long I take!''

"Elliot, that's just Sam's vain attempt to make an impact on you, and at least for that moment, he feels that he's in control again.''

"Well, when he does that, I just listen to him go on and on. When he's finished, I go on about my business. I don't let it affect me.''

"That's got to make him feel more out of control. Then he'll get more heavy-handed. He'll complain more about little things.''

"Maybe so, but I just can't let him affect me. I'm sorry. That's the way I am. That's the way I've always been, as long as I can remember.''

Elliot stopped a moment. "Wow. I haven't thought about this for years. My grandmother always told me, 'Never let things bother you.' Good grief, I just thought of something. I was in the sixth grade and some white kids started calling me 'nigger.' I remember, I went home and cried to my grandmother. She said, 'You don't have to bow to them, and you don't have to fight them. Just ignore them. If you pay any attention to them, you give them power. Just do your work. Be better.' That's exactly what I did. I did my work and I was better. The people who didn't give me trouble got all of me. The people who gave me trouble, I ignored.''

"That principle certainly has worked for you,'' I commented. "But you may be excessive with it. Ignoring people can drive them up the wall. It can make them feel powerless, like there's no way to get to you.''

"Sure there is,'' Elliot replied confidently. "Just tell me what problem you want solved. Tell me where you want me to help you. But don't try to get to me by trying to get to me.''

"OK. If that's what it takes, you've got to let other people know. So they can understand the rules of your game.''

"That's fair enough. I can do that.''

After a few more exchanges, Elliot and I concluded our meeting. I briefed him on a forthcoming meeting the following week in which he, Sam, Nancy and I would sit down together to discuss the situation and the issues. Elliot said that he didn't see how a meeting would help, but he was willing to try it.

The next day I reported back to Sam and gave him my findings and recommendations. We started in his office and finished at lunch.

This was my summary to him. First, I told him that Elliot was not deliberately defiant or delighting in causing trouble. Elliot, from my point of view, was at a different stage in his career cycle. He wanted to be on his own. He had enough mentoring. While he was appreciative about all he had learned from Sam, he no longer wanted to be treated as No. 1 son; and he didn't want to be involved with Nancy in any sibling rivalry over Sam's affections.

Furthermore, I told Sam that Elliot had no designs on Sam's job or on stealing the minds and hearts of his people. On the other hand, Elliot was pulled in by people's need for help, especially when they came to him to solve their problems. This made him look as if he were taking over, made him look like a militant in Nancy's eyes.

I stated that while Elliot was not a militant, neither was Nancy a racist. She had a genuine care for all of her people, and she wanted to do what was right and correct, and get things running smoothly.

My recommendation to Sam was to find other ways to get out from under his routine and boring responsibilities, rather than giving them to Elliot. Because the message getting across was that Elliot was his second in command and had authority over Nancy, it became a habit to go to Elliot, whom they saw as more sympathetic. Since Elliot responded, they locked him into the role of the good father against the bad mother. And besides, a little conflict between their leaders added a little excitement to the day. It was their very own soap opera.

As I finished my summary, Sam relaxed. He said that he liked the explanation that Elliot wanted to break away from being parented. Sam said that made sense to him and that it was an acceptable reason for Elliot's actions. He could also understand why Elliot was trapped into helping people since he, Sam, had the same vulnerability.

I gave Sam one final recommendation. Elliot must be made a Director. The director title had sweeping symbolic meaning for him. It would be his confirmation in the world of upper-level executives. It would be a company-wide statement of appreciation. Without it, Elliot would not stay. I said that I would share that with Jack, the executive vice president. Perhaps he could lend his support to the title change.

As an afterthought, I told Sam that Elliot was like a beautiful colt, romping over the fields, leaping fences, with boundless energy. He wasn't wild and untameable, but the joy of exercising his energy and talent just got him into many places.

Whereas Nancy, by comparison, was a reliable, steady horse leading other horses, walking in a circle, quietly, deliberately pulling a wheel to keep things moving. With Elliot and Nancy being so different, I said that I was not surprised that they got on each other's nerves. Neither was right or wrong. They were just different. Sam and the company needed both of them. Each could not possibly do the other's job. Therefore, comparisons were pointless. But each had their own strengths and excesses.

Sam wanted to know the next step. It was simple. The three of them would meet with me two mornings, a week apart. I would discuss my findings, have them study their working styles and their impact on one another. We checked our calendars and chose the tentative dates to be agreed upon by Elliot and Nancy.

When we had our first morning meeting, there was that early morning, fresh-start feeling in the air. All four of us had our coffee in hand. There was also a feeling of expectancy, a cautious spontaneity with small talk covering our tension.

"Let me start the meeting with an explanation of the multiple-ignorance complex." They looked intrigued. "First," I went on, "there is the universal fact that people who work together, or live together, invariably misread each other's intentions. We do not know what the other people are thinking or feeling. Instead of checking, we fill in with our own guesses. After a while, the guesses become facts in our minds, and then we act as if we know exactly what's going on inside the other person. Why they're doing what they're doing. So a guess becomes a fact inside our mind, and we fight for it until the bitter end."

There were smiles of recognition.

"Even after many years, people who work together and live together have large areas of misinformation, guesses, assumptions, and unverified opinions about each other. I've found this to be true in your situation.

"Part of our purpose is to clear these guesses and replace them with verified information. To help do this, I want to introduce you to the Life Orientations Theory and Training."

I described in detail the value of taking the Life Orientations Survey so that they would have a common language and framework to make their communications more compatible.

When they had finished the survey, they analyzed their results in a workbook. They checked off their strengths and excesses and identified their missing perspective.

Afterward, I answered their questions and cleared away the puzzling points. From my experience, I knew they were scanning past events and putting a new meaning on them.

Elliot's look was intense. Sam appeared impatient. Nancy seemed totally absorbed in the system.

Then I asked for their survey results, and I wrote them, along with mine, on the chalkboard:

	Supporting Giving	Controlling Taking	Conserving Holding	Adapting Dealing
Stuart	20	(31)	[24]	15
	14	(30)	(28)	18
Nancy	18	17	(32)	[23]
	16	16	(33)	[25]
Elliot	[28]	(31)	16	15
	17	(32)	[23]	18
Sam	16	(30)	18	[26]
	13	[27]	19	(31)

113

"I've circled our first choices and put a square around our second choices. If two numbers are within three points, then consider them as equal. Remember, the top results represent our game plan when things are going well. The bottom results show our preferences under stress and conflict.

"Well, that's us," I exclaimed, "condensed into a pattern of preferences. There's the name of our game. It gives us a bird's-eye view of what's important to us, where our strengths are, the areas of our excesses, our blind spots, and how that all works when we're working together. It helps to look at how we're the same *and* different.

"As you can see, Nancy prefers Conserving-Holding. That's her first choice. She likes things orderly and systematic. That's how she runs her group. Notice that Controlling-Taking is her least preferred. Direct command is not the way she expresses being a boss. It's more through establishing a system, organizing work, and maintaining a smooth-running operation. She's less interested in starting new things, just because they're new and novel. She's more interested in getting greater efficiency out of the tried and true." Nancy was nodding in agreement.

Elliot was studying the patterns. He looked away from the board and said, "Conserving-Holding. That's my last choice—except when I'm in stress or conflict. When I'm on the move, I don't like to be slowed down—as you probably guessed by my Controlling-Taking."

He turned to Nancy, "But Conserving-Holding is perfect for your work."

It appeared that Elliot was giving Nancy some appreciation. Nancy seemed surprised that Elliot could see her point of view.

Sam was still staring at the board. He was turning his cigarette pack between his fingers like a pinwheel. Finally he said, "Looks like Nancy is the only one who doesn't like Controlling-Taking. Elliot and I are pretty close there. Who's Controlling whom?" Sam laughed. "I'm just joking. It's my Adapting-Dealing."

I said, "Sam, you do have the ultimate control as boss. You and Elliot can understand each other. You both have a sense of urgency, you both like trouble-shooting, and setting things into motion. That's one of the reasons you've worked so well together."

Elliot was quick to add, "Get one thing clear, though. Sam is boss. I respect that, and I back him up."

I agreed. "Your Supporting-Giving illustrates that. Loyalty is important to you. Having close, mutual respect is part of your game plan. I bet it really hurts you when your loyalty or integrity is questioned."

"No doubt about it," Elliot confirmed.

"Also, Elliot, according to the survey results, high on your priorities is wanting to be helpful and responsive to people."

"Wait a minute—I'm no social worker. Don't get me wrong. But I do like to help people, when they ask for it. It's really hard for me to turn anybody down when they're in trouble. I seem to take their troubles on myself."

Nancy was rapt. Her face softened as Elliot talked about his Supporting-Giving.

"Elliot's talking about the excess part of helping," I said, "doing too much of a good thing. When he jumps to rescue people from their fate, he may be going too far. How much help is enough? When do people draw us into their struggles—when they really need help, or when they just want to depend on us to do their thinking and decision-making, so they can get off the hook? Supporting-Giving is vulnerable to that. Isn't that what happened to you, Elliot—with Nancy's people?"

"What can I say," Elliot hedged. "Yes, that's in the picture—true. I guess—"

"Wait a minute," Sam interrupted. "Supporting-Giving is not my top choice, but I can get into hot water with helping people, too. I think there's a bit of the rescuer in me."

"That's probably the case," I responded. "You see, Supporting-Giving doesn't have a monopoly on rescuing. There are four ways to rescue—just like anything else. Whereas Elliot would wait to be solicited before helping, you might jump in when you see the need and not wait to be asked."

"That's exactly what I did with Frances who works for me. When her drug problem was out of hand, I didn't wait. I just took charge of the situation. She needed a family and somebody to care about her, and that was that. My wife and I didn't give it a second thought. We've raised five kids, and one more wouldn't make any difference."

Sam looked at Elliot and said, "What do you know. We're a couple of rescuers."

From Elliot's expression, I was imagining that he felt empty-handed. Sam had just pulled away the dirty-old-man rumor.

Nancy said, "Well, I'm different. I'm strictly business. It's not that I'm unsympathetic, but you can't get too involved. I try to make them think, come up with their own ideas. I'll make recommendations. I'll help them plan what they have to do, but I'm not going to do it for them."

"The three of you respond to helping in different ways. But you may not recognize each other's way of helping—or trust it. Whether it's helping, or planning, or bossing, we all do it differently.

"Generally, if people don't do things our way, we become suspicious because they don't make sense to us. And if we can't get along, we explain it away with familiar labels. 'It must be because I'm a man and you're a woman; I'm black and you're white; or I'm old, you're young; I'm a doctor, you're a lawyer.' These labels mask the real heart of our differences. Our real differences are in the way we're oriented to life.

"We use these familiar labels because they are old ways of classifying who we are and what we stand for. They give us a sharp contrast for a better sense of ourselves, but they are wedges that keep us apart.

"With the *orientations* as our way of classifying differences, we have a framework to bridge; a way to use our differences for mutual advantage—like getting us total perspective, covering our blind spots for each other, and helping each other control excesses."

Sam, Nancy and Elliot were listening to me carefully. I realized I was lecturing again. I wanted to have more participation from them.

"Well," I said, "that's more than I wanted to say. I'd like to ask each of you, what are some of your observations about your orientations?"

Elliot pointed out their differences on Adapting-Dealing, how "keeping the peace" was a higher priority for Nancy and Sam, even more so under conflict conditions. They wanted things smoothed over quickly, but Elliot said he would continue to argue his point of view tenaciously under conflict. He agreed that he worried less about harmony and much more about his accomplishments, solving problems, and doing his very best.

At that point, I called Elliot's attention to a blind spot. "You could round out your perspective by becoming more aware of your impact on other people, more aware of Adapting-Dealing. For example, my impression of you is that you are charismatic. People are attracted to you. You are direct with them, you're helpful, and you're a problem-solver. Wherever you go, or whatever you do, you'll always have people who will want to attach themselves to you—be dependent on you. Especially young black people. That's a fact of your life. It's more responsibility than you may have asked for, but it's there."

I was lecturing again, but I needed to make those observations. I had listened to them in interviews for hours. Now I needed to react and release my comments on what I had seen and felt.

Later on, we settled down to a more procedural agenda, making agreements about who could do what to avoid crossing over boundaries again. Sam and Elliot took some time to clarify what Elliot could do to help Sam, without everyone thinking that Elliot was second in command—or that he was Nancy's boss.

While Sam and Elliot worked out their agreements, Nancy listened in. She seemed relieved. Order was being restored, and the chance for harmony was a distinct possibility. Her Conserving-Holding and Adapting-Dealing were being acknowledged. She could be the kind of person she liked to be.

Three hours had elapsed since we began the meeting. Since our energy level had waned, we decided to adjourn. We were tired but invigorated.

During the following week, I met with Sam, Nancy and Elliot on an individual basis. I wanted to give them an opportunity to discuss anything with me that they might have been reluctant to discuss in the meeting. I drew them out on unresolved issues and included them in our next agenda.

One week later, we had our second morning meeting. There was a buoyancy and eagerness to work. More procedures were modified. Occasionally, Sam or Nancy or Elliot would slip back and remind us of the old complaints rather than staying with the new possibilities.

But the tension was gone and talk was about the work at hand. At times, they focused on relationship matters, to make sure they weren't working at cross purposes, or ignoring each other's game plan. As the meeting progressed, my efforts became less necessary. They were on their own. When time ran out, I made some concluding remarks, thanked them for their participation, and wished them continued success.

The following day, I reported to the Executive Vice President. The situation had stabilized. No one left, and no one had been fired.

Two months later, Elliot was promoted to Director.

11

THERE'S NO BEST GAME IN TOWN

FOUR BEST WAYS TO DO EVERYTHING

Everything we do can be accomplished four ways, one way for each orientation. For example, each of us helps others, controls, plans, decides, risks, trusts, fights, compromises, and loves in our own characteristic way, depending upon our game plan.

To illustrate this, consider the following everyday things we do. Help, Control, Plan, Fight, Compromise, and Love. Most societies and most people experience these human efforts. That is how we are the same. But how we *express* them is different. How we play them out in life creates the confusion and conflict that drains away our energy, productivity, and satisfaction.

Understanding, appreciating, and utilizing each other's game plan can remove the frustration over differences and enrich our lives.

Let us first look at the difference in the way we express helping.

FOUR WAYS TO HELP

SUPPORTING-GIVING WAY TO HELP

Jill prefers SG. If you need her help, you'll need to ask her, because she doesn't like to be intrusive. She won't offer on her own until you're really hurting. But then, she's such a caring person, almost nurturing. She'll say, "I know what's best. I can tell you the right thing to do. I know how you can try harder and be a better person as a result of this difficulty." If you need some help which doesn't meet with her standards, she'll resist. But as long as your need for help doesn't violate her principles, she's there, no matter how unpopular or difficult it might be for her. She'll support, admire, and encourage you, all the while letting you know, "I will be here if you need me." This role is that of the advisor on call.

CONTROLLING-TAKING WAY TO HELP

Ken prefers CT. If you need his help, you don't even have to ask. He gives advice freely, and will offer it at the first sign of need. If you need help, he's happy to jump in and take over for you. You'll find him eager to explain how he has successfully handled similar problems, telling or showing you exactly what you have to do. The emphasis is on the doing. Furthermore, he expects you to follow his advice; and he can be surprised, or even annoyed, if you don't take it. This role is that of the expert.

CONSERVING-HOLDING WAY TO HELP

Mary prefers CH. She helps you by a sound exploration of your problem. She has a real knack for breaking it down and seeing it for what it really is in the cold light of day. Because she can keep cool and objective, you can calm down. Slowly, new options emerge, and you begin to see that there is a way out. Because she can get you to look at the pros and cons, and at the consequences of each possible solution, she gives you a feeling of certainty about the unknown and untried. This role is that of the analyst.

ADAPTING-DEALING WAY TO HELP

Bob prefers AD. He helps you by getting you to focus on what *you* want and need, and how you can get it. He'll want to know what you think and feel about this. He wants you to find your own solution. He really knows how to listen patiently and attentively, to really "hear" you, so you have the chance to reflect and find your own solution. He isn't really concerned about the "right" thing to do. Whatever you need to do to solve your problem, he's going to ease the way. This role is that of the facilitator.

* * *

Now let's compare how each orientation goes about controlling people and events.

FOUR WAYS TO CONTROL

CONTROLLING-TAKING WAY TO CONTROL

Sue prefers CT. She controls by simply taking charge of the situation. She initiates activities and can always seem to bring up new ideas. She has little hesitation in assuming an authority role. She is comfortable running the show, and she knows how to use any power inherent in her position to direct and influence you. If you are not making things happen, she will quickly fill the vacuum. And if things aren't moving fast enough for her, she'll stir things up to get everybody going.

ADAPTING-DEALING WAY TO CONTROL

Nancy prefers AD. Her control comes from her sensitivity and awareness of what will please and placate you. By not revealing her own position too early, she exerts control indirectly by leaving you without information to know where you stand, or by leaving you with the impression that she agrees with you. This allows her time to come back later to have her own way. Her humor can distract and get you off the track from important matters. "Humoring you," as the expression goes, keeps things smoothed over, instead of clearing the air. That's control.

SUPPORTING-GIVING WAY TO CONTROL

Ted prefers SG. He controls through his expectations of high standards, directing people's sights to excellence. By expecting you to do your best and to try harder, he exerts strong control. By becoming your close confidant, and a trusted, loyal advisor, someone who is responsive to your needs, he draws you into wanting and needing that help as often as possible. After relying on that help, you can become dependent on it. You can be indirectly controlled by his support, responsiveness, and caring.

CONSERVING-HOLDING WAY TO CONTROL

Bill prefers CH. He controls through establishing many rules and regulations, having people follow forms, systems, and routines. By laying down the agenda of a discussion, and by setting up the order of doing things, his control is working behind the framework and structure of his methods. He controls others by requiring facts and concrete evidence from them to make their positions credible. He also controls by analyzing alternatives and by trying to anticipate the consequences of decisions.

* * *

We all look ahead. We anticipate the future. Characteristically, we plan in a way that is consistent with our orientations.

FOUR WAYS TO PLAN

CONSERVING-HOLDING WAY TO PLAN

Diana prefers CH. In-depth planning that focuses on practicalities is paramount for her. She wants the whole story, the big picture. She needs comprehensive information and relies heavily on facts to predict the future. She likes to keep her options open, and usually she will develop plan B to supplement plan A, just in case plan A doesn't work. She doesn't like to be caught empty-handed. She doesn't ignore existing resources. She knows how to build on what she already has and what already works. She doesn't want change for change's sake.

CONTROLLING-TAKING WAY TO PLAN

Dan prefers CT. He plans on the go, quickly and informally. He finds analysis and alternatives are secondary to getting something done, to the accomplishment of the task. He'll go for short-range planning, but he thinks long-range planning is a waste of time. His kind of planning is immediate and intuitive, and usually takes place at the last minute. For him, planning often consists of a discussion in an elevator just before a meeting, or of planning for a situation when already in it. He wants action plans. "Who does what, when, and what's the next step?"

ADAPTING-DEALING WAY TO PLAN

Jim prefers AD. When he's planning on his own, he finds it difficult to come to a conclusion without first getting the reactions of others. He needs to "test the waters," to get a consensus and all-around approval before finalizing a plan.

When he's planning with others, he expends considerable effort in pulling the differing points of view into a plan all can live by. He is concerned with how to get people to accept and, most important, to *follow* his plan. He has no trouble with scrapping his plan if it doesn't seem to work, and can easily shift to some mutually acceptable alternative.

Jim thinks planning should take into consideration not only facts, but how people *feel* about the facts. For him, how to implement the plan receives as much, or more, effort as does *making* the plan.

SUPPORTING-GIVING WAY TO PLAN

Karen prefers SG. She knows how to keep relevant goals in focus, making sure that the final plan is the best possible one. Her aim is an ideal model, the best of all possible worlds.

For her to involve herself, the plan must be purposeful and about worthwhile issues. And it is important to her that the others involved during the planning process keep their promises and commitments. For her, meaningful planning centers around not what is, but what ought to be. Her plans are evaluated against high standards and hard-to-reach excellence.

* * *

After reviewing the four ways to help, control, and plan, it is apparent that it is easy for us to misunderstand and be frustrated by one another. Experience reveals that we don't believe someone is helping, controlling, or planning unless they do it the way we do it. We'd bet they just don't do those things! Or, if they do them differently, we may admit they do them, but it just doesn't seem like helping, controlling, or planning. Why would anyone want to do it *that* way?! They must be confused, inadequate, or dumb!

One other consideration emerges. If we want help, if someone is required to have control over us, or if they must plan for us, we want it done the way we ourselves do it! If it isn't our way, we may not understand or appreciate the fact that it is being done. This leads to disappointment and confusion, often resulting in a misunderstanding. Our way of helping, controlling, or planning is recognizable, understandable, and meaningful. However, only doing things our own way is limiting, and we miss out on many new and useful resources and relationships.

Next, I will describe how we fight, compromise, and love—all in our own characteristic way, according to our orientation. Here again, differences provide us a fresh way of doing something, or they can upset our efforts, depending upon our willingness to deal with those differences.

FOUR WAYS TO FIGHT

Fighting is fun for one, frightening for another. Some of us fight for principles. Some of us fight with facts. Some fight at the drop of a hat. In describing individual differences in fighting, let's consider strength and excess.

SUPPORTING-GIVING WAY TO FIGHT

Hal prefers SG. When discussions get hot and heavy, he's willing to extend himself to do what he sees as right and fair for you. Because he feels a commitment to establishing cooperation, he can be vulnerable to giving in to you rather than being seen as uncooperative. All too often, in the excess, he can become self-denying, and he can make too many concessions. He tries to influence you through statements of fairness and principle. Sometimes, he can get moralistic or self-righteous. He can make you feel guilty by conveying that he is a victim of injustice. He can display hurt, disappointment, or downright martyrdom.

CONTROLLING-TAKING WAY TO FIGHT

Donna prefers CT. She is quick to defend her territory and prerogatives. No one's going to push her around. She is firm and very clear about where she stands. She can come on so strong at times that she can become demanding or arrogant, and *you* can feel pushed around. She can be so quick to protect her rights and interests from exploitation, that sometimes she's over-vigilant and combat-ready, making you feel defensive. In a dispute, she finds it difficult to stop, but she persists until the air is cleared. This can cause you to feel under the third degree as she presses and probes for answers. You can feel yourself without breathing room to react in your own characteristic way.

CONSERVING-HOLDING WAY TO FIGHT

John prefers CH. The byword for him is tenacity. By sticking to his guns he demonstrates conviction, but when done to extreme, you can experience him as unbendable or stubborn. In fighting, he tries to be reasonable by relying heavily on facts to document his position. In excess, this focus on facts can be burdensome and make you feel frustrated with needless detail.

When the atmosphere becomes emotional, John tends to wait until cooler heads prevail before trying to settle the issue. Because of this waiting period, it appears that he doesn't care. He can become aloof and distant, not giving you the satisfaction of sustained effort, or the satisfaction that your position has affected him one way or another.

ADAPTING-DEALING WAY TO FIGHT

Judy prefers AD. When she is fighting, harmony is her overall concern. As a result, she has a willingness to understand and weigh both sides of the argument, to find a mutually satisfactory solution. But after awhile, this can lead to vacillation and inconsistency, giving you the impression that she doesn't stand up for her convictions. Judy has a hopeful, optimistic, and enthusiastic attitude that things can be worked out. Sometimes, though, she may make you feel that she doesn't fully understand or appreciate the seriousness and difficulty of the problem.

During a disagreement, she makes an effort to smooth things out quickly, and to keep the tension low through humor. This, in the excess, may prevent objections from being fully expressed, and so the air is not cleared. Then the problem will reappear at a later time.

* * *

After a fight comes compromise. Each of us has our own way to resolve differences through some kind of give and take.

FOUR WAYS TO COMPROMISE

ADAPTING-DEALING COMPROMISE

Glen prefers AD. His motto is everybody can win in a compromise. Preventing unhappy losers is his goal. He believes that winning at somebody else's expense just sets up a personal contest which will appear repeatedly during future disagreements. And he doesn't think winning should become more important than finding a compromise.

In a disagreement, Glen is willing to go along and make amends, this time, in the service of getting along. Keeping the action flowing is important to him, so he looks for a solution that will keep everybody happy. He doesn't want disagreement to develop into a running battle. He is always open to new ways to overcome an impasse, demonstrating his flexibility.

SUPPORTING-GIVING COMPROMISE

Sandra prefers SG. Compromise is possible with her only if it does not violate some principle. If she sees the solution to a problem as fair and just to all concerned, then compromise can follow. The needs of others are a vital concern of hers, and if she sees you as needy, you will get your way. One of her needs is to be seen as cooperative and worthwhile, and her way to fulfill this is to be responsive to the needs of others. In seeking a solution to a disagreement, a satisfactory compromise may not be enough for her. In compromise, as in other activities, she must find the very best solution possible, the one that holds the highest ideals and purpose for everybody.

CONTROLLING-TAKING COMPROMISE

Sam prefers CT. For him, compromise equals a hard bargain, a competitive give and take. The only worthy adversary for him is one who will wrestle through to a compromise, staying in the contest every inch of the way. He just can't respect backing down or giving in. Rather, he admires and appreciates sparring on an equal basis through the whole negotiation.

Sam is more prone to compromise when a solution is urgently needed, and time is running out; or when there is a chance of losing an opportunity. If the compromise centers around who is going to be in charge, as it frequently will, then responsibility should be divided, providing separate areas of autonomy. If this isn't done, Sam is susceptible to continually fighting for control. Splitting the territory is far more acceptable to him than is having to be under someone else's rule.

CONSERVING-HOLDING COMPROMISE

Valerie prefers CH. She thinks logic and reason are the pathways to compromise. In working to find a solution to disagreement, she takes all the alternatives and thoroughly explores them. She's good at forecasting the consequences of each option, which helps lessen some of the uncertainties.

By keeping her emotions at a low ebb, she helps to assure that the situation doesn't get out of control. She uses rules of order and a well constructed outline or agenda to serve as a map, helping her to navigate through the "troubled waters."

With her, solutions should be implemented in phases. After some proof of a successful trial, then larger steps can be taken to eventually solve the entire disagreement.

* * *

Through all of our fights and compromises, love can keep us together. But there are—yes—four ways to love.

FOUR WAYS TO LOVE

SUPPORTING-GIVING LOVE

Joe prefers SG. His heart and mind is filled with ideal expectations. High hopes, promises of loyalty, and long-term commitment are central for him. Love is togetherness, doing things together is an ideal. Love is forever.

Giving of himself and doing for you is his way. But at times, his giving too much can trigger in you feelings of being overwhelmed, indebted, and guilty for not being able to return the "goodness." Sometimes that sense of obligation can make you feel distant and resentful for not being able to measure up to that standard of giving.

The person who loves this way is admiring and adoring of you. Trust and belief in you are freely given, but if you fail to live up to the trust, then what develops are feelings of disappointment or betrayal. When there is a loss of innocence and illusion, the fall is disheartening, and trust in you takes time to be re-established. Time is also needed to push out the hurt and heal the wounds of unfilled, if not unstated, promises. Underlying all of this is a basic love premise, "To get love, I have to give it. I hope to be rewarded in kind for my loving acts, but I'll gladly make the sacrifice if they are not."

CONTROLLING-TAKING LOVE

Lisa prefers CT. For her, passion and excitement fill a bottomless vessel of desire. More is not enough. But her intense love burns brightly until the novelty wanes. Then there is a sudden doubt. Is it love after all? If it is love, then why is the flame flickering?

She gives little thought to the impossibility of such sustained passion. In order to sustain it, distance and alienation must separate her from her lover. Then she can have the ecstacy of reuniting, of kissing and making up, of going through the cycle again and again. Sometimes the ups and downs are with the same person, sometimes it is with the added novelty of a new partner.

The wooing and winning are key satisfactions in this kind of love. Feeling in charge of the relationship is also a substantial requirement of continuity.

The Controlling-Taking lover wants surprises and unpredictability in the relationship—anything to keep it from becoming routine. They will expect enthusiasm and excitement from you, not realizing that this requirement is reciprocal.

In this way of loving, there are contradictory needs. On the one hand, there is the desire for someone who will have the vitality and spirit to spar on an equal basis, stand up for themselves, and spark off energy to fuel the intensity. On the other hand, there is a need to be supported and followed, to be softly nurtured. The implicit need here is for you to value both Controlling-Taking and Supporting-Giving love. Their underlying premise here is, "I can take all that you can give, and when I get what I need, I can be free and generous to give you what you need."

CONSERVING-HOLDING LOVE

Ray prefers CH. His is a calm, cool, and collected love. He doesn't think there is much sense in wallowing in sentimental and emotional fantasies with you. He believes that if you keep your feet on the ground, the relationship can take its natural course. There's no sense in rushing things. By using his head, he thinks that he will insure a lasting and solid relationship based on reality and reason.

Because there is a quiet reserve in this way of loving, it is easy to assume that the love doesn't run deep. On the contrary, though there may be fewer demonstrable acts, the feeling for you can be intense. The expression of the feeling is the only thing that may be limited.

But the expressions of love will find their way out in many practical acts. "Little things mean a lot." Doing everyday things will have considerable meaning for them. They are expressions of care and love.

At times, because the expressions of love are indirect and practical, the care implicit in them may not be seen or understood by you. Depending on your orientation, you may want some sudden, sentimental, or playful display of emotion and affection. But this is not likely to happen frequently. Their underlying premise in loving is, "If our love meets the test of time, you will get all the love you need; we've only just begun."

ADAPTING-DEALING LOVE

Beth prefers AD. Hers is a sunny kind of love, light and airy. Fun and friendship often cover the seriousness underneath. Being casual, off-handed, hides the vulnerability and concern about losing the other person's approval or love.

Pleasing is her main course of action. She has a willingness to try anything to keep you happy. No effort is too great or too small if it pleases you. Often her efforts will be dramatized to make sure you're getting the message. Overtly, her display of feeling is enthusiastic and happy-go-lucky.

For her, doing things and going places together is a big part of the partnership. Playing together is also important.

She uses the light touch of humor to soothe you, even when the gaiety can be concealing hurt or worry about the relationship.

If there is a lover's quarrel, those with this orientation will make a quick attempt to patch things up or make amends. As a result, some vital issues about your relationship may not be given a sufficient airing, and they can pop up continuously, because they may have been smoothed over hurriedly.

When this lover goes too far, you can feel manipulated, cajoled, and distracted from serious concerns. There are times when you may denounce the ease and flexibility, and wish your lover would take a stand, and would take *more* responsibility in making decisions.

When you are in low spirits, they will make an effort to pick you up. If you are in a troubled mood, they will be concerned that harmony is slipping away, and they will make an attempt to rescue you from the bad feelings which could upset the relationship. The underlying premise in loving this way is, "Live, love, laugh, and be happy."

As you read through the descriptions above, you may have thought that one was not enough to fully describe you. That's an accurate observation. You may have realized that you were a combination of two. Many of us have more than one preferred way.

In addition to helping, controlling, planning, fighting, compromising, and loving differently, over our life span we live out the stages of our life according to our orientation.

Quite individually, we cope with breaking away from the family, establishing ourselves in the adult work world, finding a mate, creating a family, relating to children, having affairs, divorcing, retiring, aging, and dying.

As outlined on the following pages, these major events are handled characteristically, depending on our preferred orientations.

DIFFERENCES IN LIFE STAGES

FAMILY BREAK-AWAY STAGE

SUPPORTING-GIVING:

- Needs justifications.
- Finds substitute family.
- Transfers dependency to an ideal.
- Open feelings of guilt.

CONTROLLING-TAKING:

- Sharp confrontation.
- Leaves old loves for new.
- Activity hides anxiety.
- Guilt projected in fault-finding

CONSERVING-HOLDING:

- Slow transition.
- Holds onto old ties, slowly building new ones.
- Dutiful and aloof.
- Guilt rationally contained.

ADAPTING-DEALING:

- Lives in two worlds.
- Extends family feeling to friends.
- Doesn't want to cause displeasure.
- Guilt hedged by humor.

FINDING WORK STAGE

SUPPORTING-GIVING:

- Choice based on idealism.
- Waits for sponsor, a new parent model.
- Grateful for opportunity and support.
- "I want to make a contribution."

CONTROLLING-TAKING:

- Investigates opportunities and competition.
- May be scattered with too many choices.
- Volunteers self, gets in.
- "I want my own show."

CONSERVING-HOLDING:

- Fully surveys the facts.
- Takes time to decide.
- Future defined and programmed.
- "I don't want to move until I'm ready."

ADAPTING-DEALING:

- Talked into what's popular.
- Flexibility can lead to quick success.
- Finesses authority, plays their game.
- "I want to fit in."

MID-CAREER STAGE

SUPPORTING-GIVING:

- Develops self and others.
- Never meets high self-standards.
- Devoted and dedicated, lives it.
- Later, slow disillusionment, "Will I be unappreciated?"

CONTROLLING-TAKING:

- Get ahead, get the most.
- Dramatic accomplishment.
- Move or get out.
- Most important thing in life.
- Later experiences, "Now or never."

CONSERVING-HOLDING:

- Systematic, steady achievement.
- Few changes or chances.
- Thorough development of each position.
- Later can feel, "The grind."

ADAPTING-DEALING:

- Well thought of, liked by people.
- Aware of sensitive issues and relationships.
- "How can I please?"
- Later can feel, "Who am I?"

THE SPOUSE STAGE

SUPPORTING-GIVING:

- Encourages mutuality.
- Respectful and admiring.
- Resentful when not appreciated.
- If I give, I'll get.

CONTROLLING-TAKING:

- Sees as asset in career.
- Exciting and adventuresome.
- Resentful at attempts to dominate.
- If I get, I'll give.

CONSERVING-HOLDING:

- Anchor, source of stability.
- Calm, cool and collected.
- Resentful with demands for emotional display.
- I'll give to preserve what I've got.

ADAPTING-DEALING:

- Companion and social partner.
- Playful and lavish.
- Resentful if pleasing doesn't please.
- I'll get, if I please.

THE PARENT STAGE

SUPPORTING-GIVING:

- Helpful advisor.
- Teaches consideration of others.
- Disciplines by reacting to violated moral principle, behind the action.
- Desires to instill lasting values.

CONTROLLING-TAKING:

- Provides challenge for achievement.
- Tells to stand up for rights.
- Disciplines with punishment related to action, and sets limits.
- Expects performance, be a winner.

CONSERVING-HOLDING:

- Attentive but not demonstrative.
- Be unemotional and follow the facts.
- Disciplines with silent treatment or detached punishment.
- Wants thinking, rule-abiding behavior.

ADAPTING-DEALING:

- Children together, fun, good times.
- Be nice to people so they'll help you.
- Discipline by bribe, cajoling, few limits.
- Hopes for pleasantness and getting along.

THE DIVORCE STAGE

SUPPORTING-GIVING:

- Self blaming.
- Guilt over abandonment.
- Gives everything away.
- Shows hurt, surrenders.

CONTROLLING-TAKING:

- Blame projected.
- Guilt suppressed by action.
- Fights against exploitation.
- Denies hurt, shows anger.

CONSERVING-HOLDING:

- Blame avoided.
- Guilt rationalized by thought.
- Thorough, detailed accounting.
- Holds in hurt, withdraws.

ADAPTING-DEALING:

- Shared blame.
- Guilt placated by niceness.
- Friends work it out.
- Covers hurt, smiling through.

THE UNCOMMITTED STAGE

SUPPORTING-GIVING:

- Romance and togetherness.
- "Someone may need me again."
- Love conquers all.
- "I'm lovable!"

CONTROLLING-TAKING:

- Adventure and experimentation.
- "I'm not satisfied so I'm justified."
- Opportunity only knocks once.
- "I'm competent!"

CONSERVING-HOLDING:

- Practical and distant.
- "After careful analysis, I'm not ready."
- You have to build for the future.
- "I'm rational!"

ADAPTING-DEALING:

- Fun and games.
- "We really inspire each other."
- Live a little.
- "I'm liked!"

THE GROWING OLDER STAGE

SUPPORTING-GIVING:

- "Has it been a worthy life?"
- Inevitable and saddening.
- "Have I done right by others?"
- "Have I been a giver or martyr?"

CONTROLLING-TAKING:

- "Has it been a productive life?"
- A challenge to keep fit.
- "Have I done it all?"
- "Have I been a winner or loser?"

CONSERVING-HOLDING:

- "Has it been a useful life?"
- Take it slow and easy.
- "Have my plans been fulfilled?"
- "Have I been steadfast or just stubborn?"

ADAPTING-DEALING:

- "Has it been a notable life?"
- You're as young as you feel.
- "Have I kept things smooth?"
- "Have I been known or obscure?"

THE RETIREMENT STAGE

SUPPORTING-GIVING:

- Easily depressed.
- Reliance on children.
- Takes up long-desired interests.
- Lets things happen.

CONTROLLING-TAKING:

- New last adventure.
- "See, I still can perform."
- Need for self-sufficiency.
- Makes things happen.

CONSERVING-HOLDING:

- More of the same.
- Resigned and cautious.
- Planned and saved for it.
- Makes the most of it.

ADAPTING-DEALING:

- Whatever I'm supposed to do.
- Enthusiastic.
- Let's do it together.
- Makes things pleasant.

It's not easy to see our differences. When we like people and love them, we often take them for granted. We're so familiar and close, much of our thinking about them merges into a blurred photograph in our minds. We lose sight of their uniqueness and the special ways they prefer to do things. And although we know they are different from us, we still assume that they are really just like us. Love like us, plan like us, and help like us. When reality strikes us because of some disagreement, we try to convince them that our way is the best way—and all too often, the "only" way.

Without an appreciation for what those differences can do to enrich our lives, we allow our different ways of helping, controlling, planning, fighting, compromising, and loving to frustrate us and finally to alienate us from each other.

We can often find ourselves arguing over the issue of your way or my way. Are we going to follow your urgency to get things done, or my desire to go slow or be sure? Are we going to follow your need for the very best possible solution, or my need for quick results? Are we going to follow your way of sticking to the tried and true, or follow my way of trying the new and novel?

If we stop the contest over your way versus my way, we could use each other's differences to cover our blind spots and counterbalance our excess. None of us has total perspective. We could have more information about what's going on about us, and we could make fewer mistakes and add opportunities to our lives that we would ordinarily overlook.

But we still seek out people who are similar to us. We have something in common, and this similar way of getting things done makes us feel more comfortable. We feel confirmed. It is easier for us to trust the person. We know things will be done the way we like, our way—the "best" way, the "right" way.

Even for those who prefer the same orientation, conflict can occur—not as a result of their differences, but because of the competition arising from their similarities. Competition develops not from your way versus mine, but from who will get the chance to exercise the same strengths and receive the satisfactions from it.

If we are both Supporting-Giving, our conflict can be over the issue of principles. Are we going to follow your principles or mine? One might say, "My principles are higher than your principles!" If we both prefer Controlling-Taking, we agree it is time for action, that we have to move ahead—fast. But I say we should go in direction A, while you say we should go down road B.

When both of us are Conserving-Holding, the disagreement is over whether my plan or yours makes more sense. Who's plan is more thorough and reliable, mine or yours?

If Adapting-Dealing is our common ground, we can center our "differences" on who is more aware of other people. Who knows better what will please others, me or you?

Whether the same or different, there is no guarantee that we will be conflict-free. There is no guarantee that we will be compatible. Similarity, though, does make trust easier, because it is easier to understand the same orientation. With differences in orientation, it makes it more difficult to trust because we don't trust people whom we don't understand. These differences make us feel misunderstood, unaccepted, and distant.

Differences make us feel that we're not playing the same game. It's as if we are going to play in a national championship, but one team wants to decide the championship by playing football, the other team wants to do it playing baseball. Which is it going to be, our game or their game? It better be our game because it's what we know best. Their game scares us; we don't fully understand it. We seldom experience satisfactions from it, and we're not sure we can even play it!

To make our lives more productive, harmonious, and frustration-free, we need to deal with differences. There are five key steps to help us do so.

FIVE STEPS IN MANAGING DIFFERENCES

1. *IDENTIFY* differences by using the Life Orientations Survey, or by learning to observe people with your new knowledge of orientations.

2. *UNDERSTAND* how differences work for others by thinking about them and asking people about their differences.

3. *APPRECIATE* and value differences with an accepting attitude about the uniqueness of others, the four ways to do everything.

4. *UTILIZE* the differences to better plan, problem solve, and decide from a position of total perspective.

5. *ORGANIZE* activities into parts so that we each can do our part using our own strengths.

It is a marvel of human nature that we can all do the same job, be in the same organization, or be in the same family, and be so different. Vive la différence! Ah, but wouldn't it be nice if you did things my way!

12

THE CASE OF THE PERFECT PERSON AND THE JOKER

The two people involved in this case represent a clear contrast in orientations, strengths, and excesses. Because of their differences, they are able to see each other's excesses and blind spots. They represent the opportunity we have to be useful to each other when we are different.

I have also included some of my private thoughts during the session. Share in their discoveries about themselves, their brief adventure with their strengths and excesses. You might make a discovery, too.

Joan and Larry are friends. They both teach school, and they are both writers. They came to my offices to explore more about themselves, as part of their studies, and to find out about LIFO Training for themselves.

Joan has blue intense eyes. She is small and delicate, quiet but commanding. She has been introspective for some time, exploring her direction as a person and professional. As a teacher, she has instituted special programs for handicapped children.

Larry is slight, with curly black hair. His boyish face responds to his rapidly changing thoughts, ranging from devilish to peevish to almost serious. In his work, he has been able to enter cultures that have never taken in outsiders.

Notice how Joan's and Larry's seemingly casual remarks in the beginning expand and repeat all through the session, revealing important concerns about their productivity and satisfaction. As the session progresses, and they respond to the framework of LIFO Training, notice how reluctance recedes, and how evasiveness is put aside as they face important questions for improving their lives.

LIFO Training is conducted often in group workshop sessions. At times, sessions are between two people, husband and wife, parent and child, teacher and student, or people who work together. Other times, the sessions are with one person.

Joan and Larry begin the session by reviewing the 15 questions about their strengths, as you did in the beginning of the book. Then they take the 20-minute LIFO Survey. This gives them a precise reading of their preferences.

Stuart: Today we will focus on our strengths, what makes us as successful as we are, and our excesses, which keep us from moving up to our next level of success. We will also look at our blind spots that cause major mistakes in our lives and make us overlook important opportunities. In the Discovery Workbook on page 3, are 15 important questions about our lives which will help us focus our effort together. Select four questions that you think are particularly important to you.

(I look at their faces respond to the questions, a smile, some puzzlement, a frown.)

Larry: All of the above.

Stuart: See if you can discipline yourself. Select only four.

Larry: Is that a challenge or a threat?

Joan: In other words, the ones you consider top priority should be those you haven't yet solved on your own.

Stuart: Not necessarily. Just whatever criteria *you* want to select them for. For whatever reason they're important to you.

Joan: What if you're not a groupie, Stuart?

Stuart: Well, then don't consider questions 13, 14 and 15 about groups.

144

Joan: I'm really not interested in groups.

Stuart: All right, give me the questions.

Joan: 5. What new approaches to people and problems do I need to try.

          6. What kinds of pressures and conditions create stress for me.

          8. How can others help me spot where I exaggerate my strengths and help me curb their excess use.

          10. What new relationship strategies will assist me in influencing key people in my life.

Stuart: Larry, what are your four?

Larry: 4. What kinds of people will supplement my approach.

          5. What new approaches to people and problems do I need to try.

          6. What kinds of pressures and conditions create stress for me.

          9. What is the best way to supervise and manage me.

Joan: Oh, I know the "best way to supervise and manage" you, Larry.

Larry: Tell me what to do and make me do it?

(We all laugh. Joan smiles knowingly that Larry has some awareness of that question.)

Larry: Many of these I believe I understand, but I only understand them from my past experience. I feel I know what kind of people I work best with. But I would be interested in pursuing these things. I get different opinions from varying persons with whom I work. What I should be doing, what I shouldn't be doing. They all vary, and I listen, with rapt attention.

Stuart: Are you saying you may listen with rapt attention, but you do not necessarily execute their recommendations?

Larry: Of course not. Joan even tried to organize me once, "What you need is . . . "

Joan: You hate being yacked at . . .

Larry: No, I love it!

Stuart: Oh, then that's the best way to supervise you?

(Why is Larry bobbing and weaving? But it's too early to confront him with it. I'll wait to see if it continues.)

Stuart: So Joan, you—or both of you—checked off No. 6. "What kinds of pressures and conditions create stress for me."

Larry: I find it hard to find situations of stress in my life. Everybody talks about it, but I find it difficult to find those things. Maybe if I identify some of those things I might be able to handle the situations of *other* people, that is.

Stuart: For *their* stress.

Larry: Possibly. Not entirely. I get coming at me a lot of things like: "Well, doesn't that bother you? Doesn't this?"

Stuart: Those things that are stressful for other people are not for you?

Larry: Not normally.

(He's still dancing around. I'll follow him until we get in step.)

Stuart: So people experience you as neutral, like: "How come you're not excited? The school's burning down and you're joking."

Larry: Wonderful. Good example.

Stuart: They would be reflecting their impression of you as disengaged.

Joan: You push away, Larry, when you feel yourself getting engaged. I've watched you. You get very frightened sometimes.

Larry: *I* don't think I do.

Joan: You push away deliberately from fear of getting too closely involved. I've noticed that about you.

Larry: It isn't a conscious thing with me, if I do that.

Joan: Then you turn it into a joke. When anything gets too close, you defensively joke.

Stuart: That may be his orientation, his way of coping.

Larry: But also, I'm thrilled by being able to . . .

Joan: Manipulate.

(Gotcha! Does she want him to see that he's been a "bad boy"?)

Larry: No, I don't consider it that. It's seeing a response that normally they wouldn't have had, unless I would have, in some way, brought it about. Not that I have to control it, but I enjoy people getting into these little situations where they have to explore.

(He seems delighted. Does he like to make mischief?)

Joan: You start trouble, in other words.

Larry: No, I don't really, but I like to see them explore. Honestly, I'm interested in them exploring these things that they've never possibly considered before.

Stuart: So you like to have an impact on them?

Larry: Not necessarily.

(I missed. I'll try again.)

Stuart: No? You like to watch them work themselves out of a new situation. You like to be an observer, to watch their reactions?

Larry: I like to identify what I feel is a quality of their own, that they may not particularly recognize or understand. I'm around students a lot, you see. They provide excuses why they didn't get their paper in. I enjoy, I think, in a certain sense, having them look at *why* they really didn't get that paper in. I mean, I could care less, but I play little games with them. They come and ask: "Well, I'll need an incomplete." And I'll say: "Well, I'm not so sure I'm ready to give you an incomplete." Probably you could use the word "games."

(What is he trying to accomplish? It seems to keep people off balance.)

Stuart: Well, I guess what I'm sensing is that you like to be unpredictable.

Larry: Exactly. I used that in an article I wrote recently called, "Expecting the Unexpectables." It feeds my mind. Is that clear? I'm usually not too clear.

(You're telling me.)

Stuart: Yes, that's clear.

Larry: But it's funny, let me add another thing that I want to clarify.

(Watch it, here comes another attempt to cloud what's clear.)

Stuart: No, don't clarify, you'll obscure it.

Larry: Not necessarily. People accuse me of what Joan accused me of doing. I sometimes feel my humor, or whatever it's called, is where I enjoy making people feel comfortable. Quite often the humor is a very serious thing for me. And it's not a thing that's to be taken lightly.

Stuart: That's a marvelous expression, an irony. "I take my humor seriously."

Larry: Well, "humor is not to be taken lightly" is a better analysis.

Stuart: So when you joke we better pay attention.

Larry: I don't care.

(What's he doing? I feel I'm in a dodging game.)

Stuart: Well, if we are to get your message—

Larry: Yes, of course. But then, you see, I'm backing away from what Joan says. I hear that a lot, that I manipulate. Or that I use humor. I go up so close to the core of myself and I back off. But I'm not conscious of that backing off.

Joan: What I *did* notice about you, which touched me, was things that you really feel seriously about, and the things that touch you . . . you cover them up and you back away, and you invert it somehow. You cloak it. I mean it's like you're putting out all these prickles around your sensitive points, so nobody will really get up there to you.

(Larry looks thoughtful. He seems warmed by her comments.)

Larry: See, I'm not really trying to run away from that,

whatever confrontation you're referring to there. I sometimes get bored by situations and human beings relating, and I will walk away. I've discovered whatever I had to discover. And maybe that is unfair to them, because they can't in return discover what *they* have to . . .

(He seems to be reconsidering. It doesn't appear that he wants to go further. I'll shift the focus.)

Stuart: Joan, let's hear some of the reasoning behind your choices. You selected questions 5, 6, 8, 10.

Joan: Well, question 5, "What new approaches to people and problems" I need to try. Well, frankly, I never cared *that* much about people to approach them, and I was unapproachable. Really. I mean I would stand apart from everybody.

(She does keep people at a distance like Larry.)

Larry: That's neat.

Joan: Really. That was my way. I was always apart. I was always better than everybody else. I was more able, more capable. Even in high school.

Stuart: More brilliant.

Joan: Well, I did not consider myself one of a group. I've always been protected, always been isolated, always, you know, on the straight and narrow path to whatever it was that I needed to do. As soon as I found out that there was no straight and narrow, that there was no goal, that those people who were authority figures didn't know where to turn, I felt "Why am I isolating myself?" Here I thought I was on the right road to the right goal, and there wasn't a goal. I mean, when you reached the goal, it wasn't wonderful! You always had to create a new one for yourself to be top in whatever it was you were trying to do. But it was fruitless. It was just a repetition of the same things.

Stuart: So, you need some new approaches?

Joan: Yes, I think "new approaches to people and problems." Yes, because I never looked upon people as being that necessary to me before, you see? I'm just beginning to realize that there may be people who can help me. I never was content with a people-to-people situation, really.

Larry: You know, it's very strange, if I can inject this, you translate that question a completely different way than I translate it.

(I'll have to come back to Joan's new approaches.)

Stuart: How do you translate it?

Larry: Well, "new approaches to people" almost came as a result of the fact that I don't take people seriously. Somewhere in all of my approaches is something that needs to be more of a listening person, more of a stable individual. But on the other hand, I have always needed people, I've always been around people.

(He wanted to be around people, but put them off when they were there. He's on to his excess already.)

Joan: Well, not me. I would always be the one that was too successful, too good, too many A's, and too perfect, and too . . . you know, there was nothing wrong with me. I did everything right. I did everything my teachers told me, I did everything my father told me. Maybe I had too great a sense of trust, you see.

(Such wasted accomplishment. It didn't nourish her.)

Larry: Maybe it's pleasing.

(That's not her. Pleasing is Larry's style. That's Adapting-Dealing.)

Joan: What do you mean? Pleasing?

Larry: You found it very necessary to please these people by getting these top grades, you didn't dare do anything else.

Joan: I didn't do it please, though. I thought I was doing it to be . . . to live correctly.

(That's Conserving-Holding—to be correct and accurate.)

Stuart: But who needed people, if you could do everything so easily yourself and come out right, get the results you wanted.

Joan: Well, that's it. I always knew that if I could control a situation I could manipulate anybody to my way of thinking. I would be so good and so perfect that they would never have any disclaimers against me. The teachers wouldn't dare say anything against me, no one could point a finger or anything. I was always up here. But then again, it's very lonely. It's very isolated to be in the ivory tower, really, very isolated.

Stuart: People needed to learn approaches to *you*. You didn't have to learn approaches to them.

Joan: That's right, and I had a couple of boy friends who had actually said that to me. If Mohammed won't come to the mountain, and all that business. They had to be the way I wanted them to be and they had to do what I wanted, OK? I'm always more on the receiving end in terms of who decides what to do and for whom.

(That's a lot of Controlling-Taking.)

Stuart: You prevail.

Joan: Yes, but being catered to in that way, I don't think is that good for a person. You know, you are on a pedestal but it's really lonely. And it's a bad position to be in. So anyway, the new approaches to people I think falls in that category.

Stuart: Reaching out to others instead of waiting for them to come to you?

Joan: Right. And "new approaches to problems?" I don't know so much about the problems, but I know about the people.

(I better involve Larry. Keep the participation balance.)

Stuart: What about number 8? You selected that, Larry. "How can others help me spot where I exaggerate my strengths and help me curb their excesses?" How do you relate to that?

(I want him to explore his excess humor, the evasive action.)

Joan: *(Joan jumps in.)* Well, that idea of excesses interests me, because I realize that when I do something, I do it to excess. I mean, like this whole business of doing the stories. The day and night, the month and month, and not being able to stop. I mean it was excessive. And it's the same thing when I give a dinner party. If everything isn't perfect, I won't do it at all. I mean if the crystal isn't this way, and the silver isn't this way, and the meal isn't a creative totality, I don't want any part of it.

(We're back with Joan. She wants the focus. Whatever Joanie wants, Joanie gets—that's Controlling-Taking.)

Larry: You poor kid, that's all I can say.

Joan: Yes, the poor kid. No, really, people are always asking me, my husband is always asking me: "Why does one little thing spoil it when everything else is magnificent, why can't you be gratified for the ninety-nine percent that came out marvelous? Why must you dwell on the one percent, on the blemish?"

Stuart: That's simple. Your goal is perfection.

Joan: That's good. That is so. I'm pleased that I do go to excess. And what are you laughing about, Larry?

(Here's a natural break to get back to Larry.)

Stuart: You have no excesses, Larry?

Larry: Well, I don't know what that means, to be honest.

Stuart: To have excesses?

(He's feigning ignorance.)

Larry: I do whatever I can, and I go whole hog. I don't know if I consider that excess. I love involvements whether they're personal, friend to friend.

Stuart: You never did too much of a good thing? You never overextend yourself?

Larry: Oh, I probably do, but I don't feel it maybe. Maybe I'm just completely obnoxious that way.

Stuart: Maybe one of your excesses is that you don't know your excesses.

Larry: Well, I would say treating people flippantly might be an excess. Not being serious enough, at least that's what people tell me I do to excess.

(Damn! He does know his excesses. There's some competition here for control.)

Joan: Number 10, I got hung up with. "How to assist me in influencing key people in my life." I don't want anybody to help me influence key people in my life. But I would like some new relationship strategies that will help me. I don't care to influence people.

Larry: *(Teasing.)* She doesn't want to make waves.

Joan: I find that I influence people too much, just by being me.

Stuart: Most people are concerned and motivated toward influencing other people. Getting what they want from them. Everybody wants something from somebody, and if she's used to getting that, it becomes a meaningless effort for her.

Larry: I don't understand what you're saying. That's very strange, the concept of wanting something from somebody. I have trouble handling that. Couldn't it possibly be just giving them something and not caring whether there's a thing you're getting out of it?

Stuart: Well, in that case, I would define it this way. What you want from the person is to be able to give them something. You have an expectation in your giving. You want your giving to be received. That's a "want."

Larry: Wow. That falls into so many categories for me that it just . . . bamboozles my mind . . .

(He's so fascinated with that. He seems receptive now, I better get on with the LIFO Survey.)

Stuart: Well . . . this seems like a good time to take the Life Orientations Survey. It will supply you with basic information to answer the four questions you chose. It will help you collect your thoughts, organize your thinking about your strengths. It will help you discover what makes you as successful as you are, your uniqueness as a person, and how you overuse your strengths to the point of excess.

153

[Joan and Larry answer the 72 questions on the Life Orientations Survey. They tabulate their results. Twenty minutes have elapsed.]

Stuart: Now that you've completed the Survey, let me say that there are four orientations to life in LIFO Training: Supporting-Giving, Controlling-Taking, Conserving-Holding, Adapting-Dealing. Each of the orientations is like a window in a room looking out onto the world. It's as if we live in a room with four walls and four windows. Depending upon what windows we look out from, we see the world from different perspectives. Usually, we look out of one or two windows and there is one window to our back, our blind side. From a different vantage point, we all describe our partial view of the world as if it's the whole world—the only real world. Trouble starts when we try to describe to each other how things really are when we're looking from different windows.

Larry: I don't think that's a good analogy.

Stuart: Well let me finish first.

Larry: No. Let me say why, or I'll forget it. That analogy would have been a good one until Buckminster Fuller came on the scene.

(I always use this analogy and everybody says it's helpful.)

Stuart: OK, say more.

Larry: Buckminster Fuller is the designer of the Geodesic dome. He maintains that we have to get people out of the cube, rectangular thinking. We need to be in one big circular room under the dome. That's the principle of the dome.

Stuart: All right, now let me respond to that.

Larry: Now go ahead, I just wanted to give you my thinking.

Stuart: I subscribe to what Fuller is saying, that we *are* in the cube. But I'm not suggesting that that's the ideal model. I'm merely describing how we now experience our lives—inside the cube. And in fact, one of the key lessons of LIFO Training is to help people get *outside* of the cube, to see the total world from *all* windows. Eventually everybody would be out of their cube, outside of their room, seeing the total perspective, seeing 360 degrees, like from a dome. I'm trying to break down the walls.

Larry: You're just causing me to think. I'm talking out loud.

(Doesn't he mean the reverse? Isn't his "game" to make others think?)

Larry: I think there are limitations. But I mean it will work, I know, I just . . . in a certain sense I'm getting at these things just to make you think.

(I'm going to get on with the Survey results.)

Stuart: OK, Larry, what are your top and bottom results on the LIFO survey? Let's see. Adapting-Dealing is your most preferred, Controlling-Taking your second, Conserving-Holding your least preferred.

(That explains it. He doesn't like Conserving-Holding, and he doesn't like system, even the LIFO system. He wants to be free, to be flexible, do it his way—Adapting-Dealing.)

Stuart: And how about you, Joan?

Joan: Conserving-Holding is my first choice, Controlling-Taking second, Adapting-Dealing is my least preferred. And under stress Conserving-Holding is even more so.

(Interesting. Their second choice is identical, Controlling-Taking. But the most and least preferred are reversed with Conserving-Holding and Adapting-Dealing.)

Stuart: Larry, did you see how comprehensive Joan's school work was, and how organized her assignments were? Her work was a model for everybody. And Larry, your first choice is Adapting-Dealing. Wouldn't you know it, the wit and the humor, the pleasing, and . . . oh yes, working people over, playing with them, childlike at times—if not in the sandbox, in the arena of ideas.

Joan: So there!
          (*Joan caught my frustration and retaliation.*)
Stuart: The first thing to do, though, is give ourselves a
          strength bombardment. That means read about
          our strengths in the Discovery Workbook, talk
          about them, and give ourselves a pat on the back
          for them. Take time to congratulate ourselves for
          what makes us as successful as we are, our
          uniqueness . . . . Now let's look at Joan's strengths
          first. Her combination is Conserving-Holding and
          Controlling-Taking. All of these strengths do not
          have to pertain to you exactly, for you to be in that
          category. Check your Conserving-Holding
          strengths on page 11, then your Controlling-Tak-
          ing strengths on page 10.
Larry: It's weird.
Stuart: So, Larry, since your second choice is Control-
          ling-Taking, check off which of those strengths
          pertain to you. My own most preferred way is
          Controlling-Taking. One statement says, "Likes to
          be in control of a relationship and steer the course
          of what's happening." Does that click with you,
          Larry?
Larry: Definitely. Terrific. Beautiful. I don't have to go
          any further. Let's go home.
          (*Be serious, Larry.*)
Joan: Oh, yes? Are you getting too close, Larry?
Larry: "Steer what's happening." I used to be a Director
          in the theatre. Oh, "risk-taking." Definitely.
Stuart: Now let's look at Larry's least preferred
          orientation, Conserving-Holding. Being system-
          atic—orderly, take things a step at a time. That's his
          missing perspective. For both Joan and me, we
          have strong preferences for Conserving- Holding,
          while it's your least preferred way, Larry.
Larry: I agree with it. I think that *is* Joan's most preferred.
          (*I was hoping he'd focus on it being his least preferred.*)
Joan: What's that? Conserving-Holding?
Stuart: Data, analysis, logic, system . . . .

Joan:	(*Joking*) Oh, I hate that, take that away!
Stuart:	Yes, but that's you, that's what you prefer.
Joan:	No, I don't. I hate data, and I'm illogical.
Stuart:	Well, how about analysis?
Joan:	I force myself to be logical, and I analyze in a different way other than a sequential way. It's an intuitive analysis. It's a sudden illumination.
Stuart:	Yes, well feeling is data, there are all kinds of data.
Joan:	Oh, OK, as long as you say that feelings—
Larry:	Would irrationality be considered that?
	(*What's coming now?*)
Stuart:	Irrationality?
Larry:	Some creative people I know of, or with whom I deal, are fairly irrational on purpose.
	(*Here we go to generalities—not Joan and Larry.*)
Stuart:	Well, you can still be analytical and not be rigid and uncreative. I know there are a lot of creative people who work very systematically.
Joan:	No, I don't work systematically—I work by—
Stuart:	Impulse.
Joan:	Impulse. And one thing leading to the next.
Larry:	Passion.
	(*He hit it.*)
Joan:	And inspiration.
Stuart:	Oh, but Joan, look at the order in your work, the precision of your style. That is the Conserving-Holding.
Joan:	I know. And look at the preparation.
	(*Now we're moving.*)
Stuart:	OK, but the feeling and the passion of it is Controlling-Taking.
Joan:	Explain that to me. How the passion part can be the Controlling-Taking.
Stuart:	It's the force, the energy. It's the wanting to move it out to demonstrate competency; to get results quickly. And the Conserving-Holding is the

	system, the orderliness, the progression in the work. The combination gives you organized passion.
Joan:	Oh, yes.
Stuart:	And control can also come from the order and precision in your work.
Joan:	You think that? Yes, OK, OK. I understand it now, your way, all right. There's a tremendous drive and push and, yes, there's a sequence.
	(The ideas are falling into place. She's got the logic.)
Stuart:	Larry, on the other hand, has Adapting-Dealing as the *most* preferred, and that's Joan's least. Turn to page 12 and look over the different terms that describe the strengths of Adapting-Dealing for Larry.
Joan:	Oh, "personal charm."
Stuart:	His wit, right.
Joan:	And he turns it on and off. We all know that.
Stuart:	Look at the strengths stated as adjectives. "Flexible, tactful, experimental, youthful, enthusiastic, animated." Good heavens, yes.
Larry:	Not all aspects, in some I'm dying on the vine.
	(Is he starting a diversion?)
Stuart:	Like what? What do you see here that you don't think fits?
Joan:	Are you "flexible in finding ways to satisfy other people"?
Larry:	Yes.
Joan:	And you're "very quick to change and adapt"?
Larry:	Yes. In fact so much so that people can't keep up with me, and it frustrates them because I can be one thing one day and another thing another.
	(That's the excess of flexibility.)
Joan:	He's mercurial.
Stuart:	Mercurial, right. Now, with that kind of fluidity, he can shift directions much quicker than you or I could. That's a strength.

Joan: Yes, but sometimes he doesn't stop long enough.

Stuart: Now, we're not talking about the excesses. Ah, we're talking about the strengths of this style first.

Joan: Then we're going to fix him but good.

(She's smiling. Now she's getting playful. She's learning from Larry.)

Stuart: Let's bombard him with strengths before we fix him up.

Joan: Oh, yes, we have to.

Larry: I don't know if I agree with the goal, here at the bottom of the page: To be seen as "likable and popular."

Stuart: What would you say is behind your goal?

Larry: I don't know exactly.

Stuart: To fit in? That would be another way of expressing it.

Larry: No.

Stuart: Harmonious?

(Why am I playing Twenty-Questions?)

Larry: In fact, I disagree with this Adapting-Dealing process.

(Be patient. Let him challenge and resist.)

Stuart: Ah, huh.

Larry: I don't like anguish. I don't like situations which exhibit anger and—

Stuart: Ah, well, that applies to your bottom set of results of the LIFO Survey when you're under conflict or stress with Adapting-Dealing. Right now we're only considering things when they're going well, your top results of the survey.

Joan: But he says he doesn't feel that much stress, under any circumstances. Is that true?

Larry: Normally.

(We're on to something.)

Stuart: Well, that's because he reduces it so quickly with humor and the light touch, with tact and harmony.

Larry: Well, even when I'm just by myself, I don't joke with myself.

Stuart: By definition you won't. One purpose of the humor is to reduce stress, and jokes require others.

Larry: I would suppose that my goals would be more Controlling-Taking.

Stuart: Well, that *is* your second preference.

Joan: And my personal goal. If I'm truly Conserving-Holding—

           (*She took the focus away. Larry won't mind that.*)

Larry: To be seen as objective and rational.

Joan: Do I really want to be seen as objective and rational?

Stuart: Oh, yes, orderly and systematic.

Larry: No. She wants to be seen as lovable.

           (*I won't be diverted this time.*)

Stuart: Everything in its place.

Joan: *You* want to see me as lovable, Larry.

           (*She couldn't resist that one.*)

Stuart: Remember, Joan talked about being right, correct, complete. That's Conserving-Holding.

Joan: Well, I've long believed that you can't characterize the creative person as being irrational and wild and unorganized. You must have a system, a method, you have to have order.

Stuart: Even an artist who throws paint on a canvas and takes a stick to smear it into a pattern has a system.

Larry: The system of "non-system" though, Joan.

Joan: But it's not erratic.

Stuart: You're darn right.

Larry: Well everyone is erratic.

Stuart: No.

Larry: Even you, Miss Objective Rationale.

           (*He is challenging her image of herself. Is he trying to make her think, or is he just trying to be a contrary kid, or is he just expressing his distaste for Conserving-Holding?*)

Joan: Oh, well, I don't know . . . I can see what you mean.

Larry: I don't think so.

(He seems so contrary.)

Stuart: See how he toys and plays with us? His Adapting-Dealing is toying and playing. That's the inner child, his prankishness, joking.

Joan: Oh, yes, pranks, mischief-maker.

Stuart: Yes, that's Adapting-Dealing *excess*. That's the child-like aspect of Adapting-Dealing.

Larry: It's funny, as a child I wasn't that way at all. I was more like what you describe, Joan. I disgusted myself.

Joan: There's much in this description of Conserving-Holding that I would like to reject.

Stuart: What would you like to reject, for example?

(It must be the excess.)

Joan: Because I feel in my past that I have been too tenacious, practical, economical, reserved, factual, steadfast, thorough, methodical, detail-oriented and analytical.

Stuart: You're bored with it?

Joan: I'm bored with it. I want to emerge from that, Stuart.

Larry: But then what you're saying is, that's what you are.

Stuart: What would you want to emerge more into? How would you want to extend yourself?

Joan: Well, I'm waiting for *you* to tell *me*.

Larry: I've got dibs on this Adapting-Dealing.

(Now he likes it! Just before he said, "I disagree with this whole Adapting-Dealing process!")

Joan: I couldn't possibly change overnight, but I realize that even though I have won by being that way, and I have achieved success, it hasn't been a content or peaceful success.

Stuart: You paid a price.

Joan: Yes. I mean I have achieved it and "so what?" So

what have I got? OK? There's more to life.

(She really is re-examining what's important. She's at that stage in the life cycle.)

Larry: Who says you're successful?

Stuart: There he is playing again. Challenging you.

Larry: No, I'm not playing, I'm serious.

Joan: Who says? Well I don't know.

(I won't pursue that. I'll stick to her desire to change.)

Stuart: Would you like to be more of something else, or less like you are now?

Joan: In those areas where it leads to isolation, I would like for it to change. I used to be so reserved.

Larry: You are a reserved lady.

Joan: I know I am, but not as much as I used to be.

Larry: What did you call her, Stuart? Delicate and strong?

Joan: I still want to be an achiever, but I don't want to achieve at the expense of personal satisfaction and interpersonal relationships. See, I've left interpersonal relationships out of the whole thing.

Stuart: You've stayed in your own room too long.

(Oh, no. The room analogy again.)

Joan: Yes, OK, so the excesses must be dealt with. Let's see how it works.

(Good, she's ready for business.)

Stuart: Look at the excesses of Conserving-Holding for example, on page 31.

Joan: Wait a minute. I still think, Stuart, that you've got to add to that where it says "data, analysis, and logic." I don't see myself in any of those. You have to add something . . . "systematized," or "systematic," "step by step," or "building," or something like that. Because some people won't think of themselves like that at all.

(I hear you, but no diversions now.)

Stuart: Look at the excess column. Which of those would pertain to you?

Joan: No, that first one not at all.

Stuart:	How about the second one?
Joan:	"May confuse people with too many options, preventing action." Whose actions? Theirs or mine?
	(She's precise—Conserving-Holding, all right.)
Stuart:	Both.
Joan:	Yes, I tend to do that.
Stuart:	Or, "taking too much time researching, and making others feel uninterested." How about, "Not being flexible enough to provide concessions which would help solve a problem"?
Joan:	Yes.
Stuart:	Look at the adjective columns. The first excess is, "Cannot let go." Look at some of the others, "stubborn, elaborate, plodding."
Larry:	Nit-picky.
Joan:	Yes, so the strength of being "steadfast" becomes "stubborn" when pushed to excess, and "thorough" becomes "elaborate." That's me. I become elaborate. I become very over-decorated. How does "detail-oriented" come to be "nit-picky?"
	(Now we're rolling.)
Stuart:	Well, you start to check everything, dotting the i's and crossing the t's. You want everything exact, correct, no matter how inconsequential.
Joan:	For example, when I make sure all the crystal is clean, the silver is polished before a dinner party.
Larry:	Yes, that's nit-picking, yes, right.
Joan:	If you have dinner with me, would you rather look at beautiful crystal that's so sparkling and bedazzling, or would you rather look at a dirty spot?
	(Who am I having dinner with, her or the crystal? What can I say to her about her own sense of worth?)
Stuart:	If you and your spirit are compelling, I won't even see the crystal.
Joan:	But I would be the crystal then.

Stuart: Yes, exactly.

Joan: All right.

Stuart: So what are you avoiding? For people to see that you are crystal, to see inside of you? By bedazzling them with the crystal and the perfection of your table, does that obscure the beauty inside of you, or what you may feel is ugliness and not worthy of observation?

Larry: That's beautiful. He said that really beautifully.

(Larry is serious. I'm surprised, but I'm pleased with the acknowledgment. That's no laughing matter.)

Joan: About my work? Yes, he told me before about the elaboration.

Larry: No, the *crystal* example is very good.

Joan: Say it again, Stuart.

Stuart: I can't really.

(She couldn't hear me, and I can't recapture what I said. It was in the moment.)

Joan: It's a different thing from what you said before to me. It's taking it a step further.

Larry: The crystal is you.

Stuart: The crystal is you.

Joan: Yes, but the crystal is always me, but I didn't look at it so closely.

Stuart: Yes, but you as the crystal are so besmirched by thumbprints and imperfections . . . besmirched, that's Shakespearian.

(Besmirched? Where did that come from? Maybe I'm trying to be elegant with a word to recapture the beauty of what I said before about the crystal! I feel embarrassed.)

Joan: Yes, here's a mote in the eye.

Stuart: Well, see, we're thinking about your excesses.

Joan: All right, what are my excesses? Why am I besmirched? I can't stand that image that I'm besmirched and spotty and dirty. Tell me again. What are you saying?

(I hope I can recapture that. I'll try.)

Stuart:	Somehow a view of yourself has been inculcated by you and others that you as a person are far from perfect, far from crystalline. And not being able to control the inner *im*perfections, you then focused on outer perfection. If you couldn't make yourself—
	(I'm not saying it.)
Joan:	Oh, I see what you mean.
Stuart:	—worthy on the inside, you could make yourself worthy on the outside. That if every glass was spotless, every piece of silverware shined, then you're above reproach. Beyond setting a beautiful, orderly and lovely table, there is a "self-serving" aspect.
Joan:	And what's that?
Stuart:	To be OK as a person. To prove your acceptability.
Joan:	Yes, that part of it I understand. OK. But the feeling that the inner part is besmirched, that I don't feel.
	(I wish she would have heard me the first time. It was right, then.)
Larry:	You consider yourself Virgin Mary?
Stuart:	Why the drive for perfection? Not ninety-nine percent table, but one hundred percent table. Why is it that when the one percent goes wrong, you collapse, you're a failure?
Joan:	I don't collapse, but I don't feel right.
Larry:	Do you get angry, do you?
Stuart:	You didn't make your goal of perfection?
Joan:	Yes.
Stuart:	Your being perfect is out to prove something.
Larry:	Well, it's almost like the table becomes you. And maybe you have this drive to make sure that everyone sees you.
	(Good guess.)
Joan:	Oh, undoubtably, yes.

Stuart: If a person really felt perfect, they wouldn't strive to be perfect.

Larry: There is sin within you.

(Oh, he's playing again. It's hard for him to stay serious.)

Joan: Yes, but I want to know from whence it came, I don't know.

Stuart: Is it important to identify the cause of the excess to control it?

Joan: You don't think it's important to find the cause?

Stuart: I don't know. It's the question I'm raising. I'm thinking you might be able to work backwards and change your behavior without necessarily understanding the cause.

Joan: No, because cause-seeking is guilt inducing, I think.

Stuart: So if you can think in terms of *more or less,* if you can work back from over-elaborate to thorough, if you can get a quantitative sense of where the threshold is between thorough and over-elaborate, and not overuse thoroughness, you may not have to bother with getting at the cause.

Joan: But then I may not ever create again, Stuart, either.

(She's afraid to give up the excess for fear she'll destroy the strengths.)

Larry: Well, then you'd become Adapting-Dealing in the excess.

Stuart: See, everybody's fear is that if you do *less of it* you'll lose it *all.*

Larry: If you don't use it, you'll lose it.

Joan: Yes.

Stuart: But how much of a good thing is enough?

Larry: Wouldn't that vary from individual to individual?

Joan: Now you see, Stuart, I could never have done that series of stories if I had not felt tension and incompleteness.

(A diagram is in order. I'll describe excesses visually. I'll go to the chalk board and draw a diagram.)

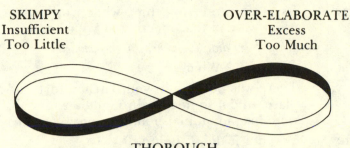

SKIMPY
Insufficient
Too Little

OVER-ELABORATE
Excess
Too Much

THOROUGH
Most Productive
Just Enough

Stuart: Here's a horizontal figure eight. In the center of
           the eight is the optimum point, your thoroughness,
           the most productive. When you go too far to the
           right, you become over-elaborate, complicated, a
           labyrinth. That confuses people, and it's an energy
           waste, too much of a good thing. If you move back
           from your excess, past the center, you go over to
           the other extreme and become skimpy and
           superficial. By not being elaborate, you wouldn't
           swing automatically over to skimpy. It only feels
           like you would.

           (I like this model. It says it for me.)

Joan: In one area, I'm superb. Organized, marvelous,
           thorough, decorative, everything. But something
           has to give, because you cannot maintain that in all
           areas of your life. Often I don't do the laundry. I
           let things pile up.

Stuart: But let's take your writing. Something that you're
           investing energy into. When you're thorough,
           you're working at an optimum. You can be
           thorough without being over-elaborate. And if you
           were to go too far in the other direction, let go and
           be sloppy, that doesn't mean you're that way
           forever. You're in the figure-eight and you would
           swing back naturally. We are a self-contained
           system with closed loops, we don't drop off the

167

end of a line.

Larry: I saw an interesting thing while working with you when we had that meeting at your home.

(Hm. They didn't comment on my model.)

Joan: Oh, really? What?

Larry: There was nothing in your kitchen that was out of place. And if somebody brought in a dirty dish, you were like an animal pouncing on its victim.

Joan: Yes, but it didn't belong.

Larry: You had to get it into that dumb dishwasher, even to the exclusion of the people. You cut the people off because the dishes were more important than the people.

Joan: Did I?

Larry: I mean, they weren't aware of it. I was just watching you.

Joan: That's what I told you before, Stuart, I either go all the way, or I don't go at all. I don't mind it when my kitchen is totally a mess. I mean if it's totally a mess, it's too far gone anyway. To heck with it. Forget about it. OK? It's either one thing or another.

Larry: But you'd probably apologize for it, wouldn't you?

Joan: No, because nobody would be there then.

Stuart: Quarantine. Joan is in disarray.

Larry: Other than that, I had dinner at your house and it was the same way. Before anybody could talk, you had to have everything cleared off, into the dishwasher, and everything plugged in and right.

(With Conserving-Holding being his least preferred, he'd notice hers.)

Joan: Yes, that's true.

Larry: Little Miss Maid, or the little Miss Servant Girl.

Stuart: Now why would Larry in particular notice all this?

Joan: Because he is Adapting-Dealing. He'd be more aware of the social aspect of what's going on.

Stuart: Yes, and Adapting-Dealing is your least preferred,

Joan. And *your* most preferred, Conserving-Holding, is his least preferred. So both of you would be attending to different things, looking from different windows, emphasizing different events and different information in the same situation.

Larry: No, sometimes I get hung up on that same thing. At one point, I was where she is. I used to have things meticulously organized, but then my family took over, and I couldn't. So I had to adapt and accept.

Joan: These are not the sort of things that I would talk about with most people, you realize.

(She's having some second thoughts about being so open, about looking good to us.)

Stuart: Yes, I understand. You're in a LIFO Training session which stimulates this kind of focus. It's a discovery experience.

Joan: Right. You see, I have realized these things about myself all along. I know that I am excessive in certain areas. I know that I give my energy totally. I'm either/or. I can't see half way with anything. There are certain things that I just have to leave out of my life, not care about, not be sociable to certain people because I can't complete what I think is the most important. OK? The excesses I already know about, it's how to go about changing.

(This is too soon for her excess. I want to confirm her strengths.)

Stuart: You could have more energy available if you didn't go into excess. You would have more time for people. But I also don't want to belabor the excesses without giving fair balance to the strengths.

Larry: Good thought.

Stuart: You wouldn't have the excess if you didn't have the strength. The excess is a natural consequence of having the strength. You wouldn't be as successful—in any kinds of terms that you want to define success. If you weren't this way, you wouldn't be you.

Joan: The other side is the fear that if one allows oneself to go off in other directions, one loses the power and the trump card. The power of that vitalizing energy that can build the strengths. One feels one can dissipate one's creativity and individuality.

(She's still afraid to let go of the excess.)

Stuart: Excess isn't the trump card. It's the joker. You don't really need it. Look at it in terms of a kaleidoscope. When you twist a kaleidoscope, you change the arrangements of the forms and the colors to create a different pattern. But you haven't thrown any of the pieces out of the kaleidoscope. You've merely rearranged the elements.

Larry: Or you've hidden some.

Stuart: Some may be suppressed under others, temporarily, until you shift the kaleidoscope again. You don't lose them.

(I hope that made sense to her.)

Joan: But, you see, even within that model, I understand what you're leading to. I understand it, but I'm thinking in my own terms. When I have suppressed my creativity in order to give to my students, or to absorb some of the brutality of their lives, I feel I've taken away something from myself in order to give to others. I feel exhausted from it. And I feel that I've betrayed myself somehow. Is that strange to you? Because, for instance, of these two years that I've spent working with the disadvantaged kids, I felt they were draining me dry, almost. They were taking from me the creative energy that I needed for myself. See, they could not nourish me. I was nourishing them, and they were depleting me. And at the same time, I could not write.

Stuart: Of course, that's perfectly understandable.

Joan: So now, like this whole year I have not taught. I've had the opportunity to dwell on myself, to be with myself, and to draw from myself without anybody to bother me, to pick at me and to drain me. I found that I've uncovered a whole lot of things about myself. And now that I've undergone it, it's like that old saying . . . Oh, what's that old expression, "If I am all for myself, what am I?"

Stuart: And, "If I'm all for *you,* what am I? I am nothing."

Larry: Oh, that's beautiful.

(Larry and I are in step.)

Stuart: I want to come back to something very important that you said. In the kitchen, the people coming over, and we talked about your all-or-none way of doing things. I think you trap yourself because you think in *either/or* terms, rather than in quantitative terms of *more or less.*

Joan: Oh, yes, I tend to.

Stuart: You say, "I gave two years to the kids, now I gave a year to myself." Sure you were depleted. Sure they took from you and had nothing to return. But during the time that you were giving and giving to them, it was really incumbent upon yourself to find, within that time frame, ways to get nourishment for yourself not by one thing *or* the other, all-giving helper and now all-taking, all-self-renewing writer.

Joan: Yes.

Stuart: Is there some way to go in and out of that? More or Less? Be a giver *and* taker simultaneously.

Joan: That's the difficulty, Stuart, because when you're involved in something like that, it's a total immersion into the experience . . . Well, how are you going to change me, Stuart?

Stuart: We're not going to change you, we're going to help you control your excesses, and re-allocate your energy and emphasis. We don't want to throw out the dishes with the dishwater. We're going to have you moderate your strengths, to prevent self-defeating action by keeping your strengths from becoming excessive.

(That's too general.)

Joan: Oh, that I know. How are you going to teach me
           to prevent this self-defeating action? Well, I'll tell
           you, you already did that one day when you called
           me up. When I told you I had gone so far with my
           writing that I had reached a peak, a climax. I hate
           to use the sexual terminology, but you likened it to
           a sexual experience, the need to continue feeling
           that climax.

Stuart: Experiencing the resolution of it.

Joan: Yes, then I know I was emotionally exhausted from
           the whole thing I had undergone, but I was still
           resisting stopping because I had reached like two
           climaxes, like I showed you the stories. The first
           should have been the climax, and I wouldn't let it
           be. I couldn't even continue that one, I had to go
           on. I mean I could not complete that one climax,
           I had to have another, which was two more stories.

Stuart: Well, we talked about gluttony.

Joan: Yes, and it made me feel, yes, it was beginning to
           be excessive. And in that sense eventually
           nonproductive, because there is a point beyond
           which you should not go. And then, that
           conversation was very instrumental in my just kind
           of tapering off. It really was.

           *(That's one answer for curbing excess—somebody has to tell
           you.)*

Stuart: So you do need people. People can help you
           control your excesses.

Joan: Then when I read my work up at the convention,
           most of the people thought it was done, finished,
           that I had made my statement. And I felt at that
           point, well, that's it. Even though there's more that
           I could have done.

Stuart: One of the excesses of Conserving-Holding is
           beating a dead horse, not wanting to stop, let go,
           keeping at it, squeezing the last bit of good out of
           something. That experience gave you a feel for
           where your threshold is when you're going too far
           and you should stop. That's a very subjective
           threshold that you could learn only yourself. Or,

you could have people watch you, and when they sense a natural closure and you're continuing, they should say, "Hey, Joan, I think it's done."...You know, there are eight personal and situational causes of stress that can lead to excess. They're listed in the workbook. One is deadlines. In your work situation, you have some tough deadlines.

Joan: Unrealistic deadlines.

(She needs to see the connection between her excesses and the situation.)

Stuart: Yes, you're going back, you're trying to meet deadlines *and* conflicting expectations. You have expectations for yourself, and they're pulling you every which way. You're in a state of overload, trying to do too many things, trying to do it all.

Joan: Definitely yes.

Stuart: Your desire for self-knowledge, self-exploration is high risk. You're in a whole new, uncharted land, yourself. You couldn't be in any more of a stress-producing situation, personally and at work.

Joan: That is definite.

(She's with me.)

Stuart: So this personal and situational stress induces excess. If you want to get rid of the excess, get out of some of the pressures, make some *decisions* about your work, get a more realistic workload. Work on the conflicting expectations, and then—puff, the excesses disappear.

Joan: Right, I know I must make those decisions, I really must.

Stuart: And the excesses in some ways become a convenient way to avoid the decisions which could resolve the cause of stress in the first place.

Joan: Right, that's largely it.

Stuart: And the longer you defer the decisions, the longer the excesses will continue.

(That's what it all boils down to.)

Joan: Larry, aren't you glad you came today?

(Why didn't she say that? It's hard for her to express appreciation directly.)

Stuart: Now, if you want, when you go home, you can do the exercises on pages 45-48 of the Discovery Workbook, thinking through those excesses and coming up with an action plan, and committing to paper some small plan for correcting the source of the stress.

(Larry's been quiet. He hasn't interrupted us.)

Stuart: . . . Now I'd like to talk to Larry about other people's view of him. Sometimes he may come across as if he's not involved, or doesn't care.

Larry: Or, just the opposite of that. There are people who are afraid of me.

(He's taking an opposite position again.)

Stuart: Oh, afraid of you.

Joan: I feel the opposite. That you become afraid.

Larry: Of them?

Joan: Not of them — of developing yourself.

Larry: I'm not conscious of that, but I may be.

Joan: I feel you're protecting something vulnerable.

(She's picked up something.)

Larry: Could be, I don't know.

Stuart: Well, let's look at that for a minute, the excesses of Adapting-Dealing.

Joan: And you manipulate others because of it. Not with me, though.

Larry: Oh, yes, I would do that with you.

Joan: You would?

(Joan seems disappointed. We could explore that, but now Larry's excesses have priority.)

Stuart: Look at page 32. The Adapting-Dealing excesses.

(Larry is nodding his head.)

Larry: I can identify with every one of these. Where I get confused with myself is where it says, "Becomes

174

overly entertaining and distracts from the seriousness of the situation." I have a very thin line between what is serious and what is humorous. And that's where I think it gets me into trouble, because the people with whom I associate don't have those same divisions.

(He's owning up to his excesses.)

Stuart: Well, one of the strengths in Adapting-Dealing behavior is that when other people are taking things too seriously and everything seems a matter of life or death, you come in with humor and break the tension, and put some perspective on it. Like, "This isn't a matter of life or death. Come on, now, this is just another day with another problem."

Larry: Right!

Joan: Yes, you see we need people like you. *I* need people like you.

Stuart: Right:

(We've come a long way.)

Larry: Well, I sometimes resent that, though, because I become someone that other people manipulate.

Stuart: In what sense?

Larry: The department chairman called me—

Joan: Like they don't take you seriously?

Larry: No, no, that's fine. I don't care about that. For example, the department chairman called me and said: "Would you come to our party because we want the light touch?"

Stuart: He actually said that?

Larry: As though I'm being used to manipulate on behalf of someone else. It's their goal which I'm supposed to handle.

Stuart: Well, yes, he's orchestrating the party stylistically to make sure he has enough varieties of people to make it interesting.

(People do appreciate his strengths.)

Larry: And he was really grateful that I was there. But as I say, the only thing I resent about that is that when

	I'm placed in those positions, usually people don't care where *I'm* coming from, and I've learned through the years to just give them whatever they want me to give them.
Stuart:	Which is typical of Adapting-Dealing. To please.
Larry:	Yes, I suppose. But I kind of resent that they don't want to be interested in me, as a person, and where I'm coming from, my ideas. And so you live alone, in a certain sense.

(He doesn't appreciate his strengths because he's focused on the excess. The excess makes him feel alone in the crowd.)

Joan:	Larry, do you feel deflated? Do you feel that people are not taking you seriously, and not seeing more depth to you, is that it?
Larry:	I'm not so sure about that. No, no, that doesn't bother me, because I know that people know what my depths are. That I can handle.
Joan:	But you don't like being manipulated into the position of playing the fool?

(He likes the jester role if he's initiating it, but resents it if somebody else expects it.)

	You know, Larry, when I met you at that conference, I felt that you didn't put yourself in a position for anybody to get to know you in depth. You were like flighty, you were moving.
Larry:	Well, remember how I came into that situation?
Joan:	You were late, or something?
Larry:	Well, probably I was uncomfortable because I didn't know anybody there.
Joan:	But once you saw me, you automatically *knew* me, didn't you? Remember we took a walk?
Larry:	No, I think part of it was because you came to me.
Joan:	Did I come to you, Larry? Now that's very different for me to come to people.

(We'd better get back to his excesses.)

| Stuart: | Larry, Joan says you didn't put yourself in a position for people to get to know you. You were flighty and funny. Remember, humor keeps |

	distance between you and people.
Larry:	See, now that's an interesting thing, because people out there at the end of the humor, not myself, find distance. I find the closeness.
Stuart:	With the humor?
Larry:	Because this is where I really find out where people are coming from very quickly.
Stuart:	They may get the impression that you're taking things too lightly.
Larry:	Or, that I'm not being honest with them.

(Maybe both.)

| Stuart: | You mentioned earlier, too, that you don't like situations where there's a hassle. You're able to see both sides of an argument. It gives you a beautiful talent for taking either position in an argument, like you've done today, with us. |

(Now we're really getting into Adapting-Dealing.)

Larry:	I found in meetings of groups of people that that can be very advantageous.
Stuart:	From the strength side, it helps integrate different points of view in a situation. You can acknowledge your understanding of both positions, and bridge different ideas and different people. The excess is that people won't know where you stand, or what you stand for.
Larry:	Now, I'm with students a lot, like in South America and around the world. What I get from them in a dialogue is that I'm able to crawl out on limbs and get back very quickly and comfortably.
Stuart:	You see, with your Controlling-Taking you'll take a risk and go out on a limb, but you have so much verbal finesse with the Adapting-Dealing that you can wiggle back safely.
Larry:	Probably, yes. There is a point I want to get to. On Adapting-Dealing, it says that one excess is, "Appears so tactful that they create mistrust about their real thoughts and feelings." People have to tell me or ask me if I'm serious or not.

Stuart: There's no way of telling from the outside.

Larry: Oh, I see . . . .

Stuart: You know, in broadcasting they hold up a sign, "Applause." Well, with you, in a sense, you have to hold up a sign, "Joking."

Larry: Well, I constantly have to reaffirm to people that I am, but I don't like to, because my joking isn't joking quite often.

Stuart: They can't distinguish your intent—when your joking has a very clear and profound message, and when the joking is just to lessen the tension and be playful.

Larry: Then, on the other hand, if I'm asked to MC a banquet, I fall flat on my face, unless I'm serious. Now isn't that ridiculous?

Stuart: Tell me more.

            (He's taking down the barrier.)

Larry: I can't create an artificial humorous situation. I have to depend on the reaction and interplay. If I don't have that, I'm a goner.

Stuart: Otherwise you come off as unfunny to a large audience?

Joan: Part of his enjoyment is watching the reaction.

Stuart: And playing off the reaction?

Larry: Yes, that's true.

Stuart: I see. You don't do well in a soliloquy. You need a dialogue.

            (Of course. Humor needs an audience. How can Adapting-Dealing be expressed in isolation?)

Larry: I find a great amount of pleasure in that. I was on a bus in South America and sitting behind me was an army officer with a pistol. By the time we'd gone ten miles, I practically had his whole uniform on my body. I made a bet with this kid next to me that I could do it, see. And the only thing that I couldn't get away from him was his pistol.

Stuart: Just by kidding and cajoling?

Larry: I put my hat on his head, you know, then put his on mine.

Stuart: Oh, and you exchanged clothes?

Larry: Unrealistic!

Stuart: Well, no. Think of the child in you. If a child was sitting there and playing with this army officer, he would say, "Ah, sure, here, let's play."

(That's Adapting-Dealing, all right.)

Joan: The playfulness, see that's part of your charm, your playfulness and your whimsy.

Stuart: That's your strength.

Larry: Well, I'm trying to understand the origins of it all which probably goes back in my childbood, in being reared on a farm way out in the country where I had nobody around, no one. It was like, you know, you talk to trees. And for me it's a way of being there again, I think.

Stuart: Playing?

Larry: Yes, a great thing. But my childhood was serious. All the business about the war and my father being called up for duty. We just had a lot of unfunny things happen. There was a wreck outside our door, and I remember going to the front door and here was this man all bloody, and this was during the war. And we had all Japanese kids in our school room, so they were hauled off to prison camps. Everybody had blinds on their windows and blacked out their lights for air raids. A lot of those things happened. I think it took away the time when I should have been playing.

(His excess is trying to make up for the past. He's overloading the present with too much Adapting-Dealing.)

Stuart: You were deprived of playing, and conflict brought seriousness to you too soon.

Larry: Probably. I think I was a very serious child. Shy, withdrawn. I found great joy in being able to . . .

Stuart: Come out of that?

Larry: I didn't have anybody to relate to, see.

(You can't make up for it by playing around.)

Joan: You had no brothers or sisters?

Larry: Yes, I had a younger brother, but there was too much conflict there to be a real sharing experience.

(Is that why it was so difficult for Larry to share himself at the start of the session? I felt that competition from the beginning.)

Stuart: So what orientation does your brother prefer, do you think?

Larry: He's very dogmatic and very . . . there is one way to do everything! Controlling-Taking.

Stuart: Very interesting . . . So, what we've been experiencing today, in both your personal backgrounds, is the richness of your uniqueness . . . within the basic four orientations to life.

Larry: That's polite, but that's beautiful.

Stuart: We also have been experiencing some of the pitfalls of doing too much of a good thing, and last, the importance of thinking in terms of *more or less* about what we do, rather than all or none.

Larry: I thrive on irrationality.

(Where did that come from? What's he up to now?)

Stuart: That's the stuff of play. But I have another impression about your Adapting-Dealing that I want to share. Other people may have difficulty knowing when they are making an impact on you—positive or negative. They're off balance, trying to read you. You are in control.

Larry: Exactly. But I'd like to change that. I'd like to be allowing them the chance to know what happens.

Stuart: Where they stand.

(He really wants to curb his excesses.)

Larry: Yes. I find my students especially, my kids can handle me perfectly well. You know it's really amazing.

(Do the kids have a special affinity for Adapting-Dealing, I wonder?)

Stuart: They've seen you enough times, in enough situations to be able to calibrate you, understand you. I've noticed a number of times, when I've attempted to be very positive about you, you parry that off with a joke.

Larry: Coming from where I am, my family background, Swedish, Scandinavian, you don't accept compliments. It's that kind of thing. And you don't express any of your deeper feelings. That's the sign of weakness. And that's ingrained in you. You don't show any emotional structures.

(Hiding emotions behind his joking.)

What's so strange is people assume I'm always playing a role. I don't understand.

(Of course they do. That's the price he pays for too much joking.)

At the family picnics, we did our song and dance routine. I called them dog and pony shows. The family would show us off. The family didn't like the arts at all, or acting. They were farming people.

Stuart: You entertained them, their friends?

Larry: Yes, or the family. Families are very clannish in Scandinavia. Very hard to break into it.

Stuart: Yes, well, you said before you were a Director in the theatre. How did you get into the theatre if they didn't like acting or the arts? Did you go against their wishes?

Larry: Not necessarily, not directly. You see, I was so shy. But I always felt I was in control of my mind. It was my mind that was making me shy. So, control it, do something about it, you have to memorize lines, movement, reactions, actions, and the theatre was the best place I could go. And student government, but that was very painful, very, very painful for me.

(He trained himself for the role. He built a system to cover his shyness.)

Stuart: So you had your props for social success, for relating to people. You had your script.

181

Larry: I did yes.

Stuart: A vehicle to overcome your shyness.

Larry: The props now become the people. And they sometimes become crutches for me. I agree with you. And that's what I consciously through the years have tried to do—remove the props. But you know, you become habitually involved in relating to people, and you're always the funny guy.

Joan: Well, today you're different.

Larry: No, I'm not.

Stuart: Today, this day, you mean?

Joan: Well, a little different, yes, today.

Larry: I have had to think seriously about these problems.

            (He does have a serious side, of course. Adapting-Dealing isn't his only orientation.)

Stuart: Larry, I was very touched by what you said in the hallway to me earlier today when we were alone. I mean, I was touched two ways. Touched in the sense of your striking a responsive chord in me, and touched in the sense of making contact with you. When you complimented me on my way of giving feedback about people's problems, there was warmth and appreciation in your voice. I could feel it.

Larry: Well, you'll find probably in relating to me more, that I find it easier in a one on one, strictly one on one situation.

Stuart: So you'll be less playful, more serious and more encountering of the other person, one on one.

Larry: Possibly.

            (Oh, don't hedge now.)

Stuart: OK, so when you have more than one it becomes an audience?

Larry: And then I act.

Stuart: And then it's a family situation, right, then you do your—

Larry: Dog and pony show.

Stuart: I hear something reverberating in your description of where you are now and some of the issues you'd like to be working on. The business of your being in the theatre and not liking to play the roles, and rejecting the theatre because you felt it really wasn't you.

Larry: Well, it could have been me, but I felt it was threatening because in a certain sense it deluded me.

Joan: Diluted you, not deluded you.

(That's clever. She understands about the energy loss. The figure-eight diagram did help.)

Larry: Yes, diluted.

Joan: Yes, and that's what I feel too, about dissipating my energies on too many things. I feel diluted, right.

Stuart: So we each have a way of *diluting* ourselves. Joan with her work load and Larry with humor. Excesses dilute energies. So what we need to do is have somebody who is different from us to counterbalance our excesses, and allow them to supplement us. Larry, you need Joan to supplement you with her Conserving-Holding—your least preferred. Joan, you need to be supplemented by Larry's Adapting-Dealing, with the light touch to counterbalance you. You're a perfect complement for each other.

Larry: Joan wants me to finish my school project, you know. Well, actually, I am involved in the project in my mind. It's all up here. The organization, the structure. Frustratingly so. But, I haven't had energy and time to be able to put it all together.

(Larry, you're kidding yourself.)

Stuart: Well, that's one level of explanation.

Larry: Which means I'm going to re-identify priorities. I want to get it done, you see.

Stuart: Yes. And one of the time traps for the Adapting-Dealing orientation is that priorities can be very quickly shifting to meet the changing requirements of the situation of important people.

(That's the excess of flexibility and pleasing.)

Larry: You shouldn't be so painful.

Stuart: Say more about why it's painful.

Larry: Because what it means is you have a series of things over here. A student this, student that, you know whatever. Problems, OK, "Would you help me, I need to get into Grad school. Would you write me a recommendation?" They've been at your house, they've had dinner with you.

Stuart: Remember the Adapting-Dealing orientation says, "If I please other people and fill their needs first, then I can get the good things in life I've wanted all along." But time is running out on your project if you keep pleasing them first.

Larry: Well, I've considered myself as being gifted in a number of areas. And I probably have been playing around too long with those things, and not capitalizing on them. That's my problem . . . But Joan, why don't you accept the fact that you *are* crystal?

(Another quick shift. He won't say he's had enough. He just diverts by putting the other person in the spotlight. She loves it, though. He certainly knows what will please.)

Joan: I am accepting the fact that I'm the crystal. I believe it.

Larry: And whether you're clean or dirty, it's still crystal.

Stuart: She cares if it is clean or dirty. That's the problem—or she thinks *other* people care.

(I've fallen in with Larry's diversion.)

Joan: No, no. Because I've found out, Stuart, other people don't really.

Stuart: What do those fools know? Look at the low standards they have.

Joan: That's exactly my reaction!

(We're all laughing together.)

Larry: What do you think he said it for?

Stuart:	Is this your way of being superior? I'm OK because they're not OK?
Joan:	I suppose so, but then again . . . I mean, I consider my things, finer, OK?
Larry:	Well, *you* are superior, truly superior.
	(*Keep up the diversion, flattery will keep the focus on her.*)
Joan:	No, I don't mean to . . .you're not even listening.
Stuart:	He's listening too well.
Joan:	You're playing with me.
Stuart:	Yes, he's playing with you.
Larry:	I love to, it's great.
Joan:	I know, I know. From you, I don't mind.
Larry:	You see, Joan, I wouldn't care if you slipped and fell in a mud puddle. I'd probably laugh.
	(*I think he means it. He'd accept her for her, not for her achievements.*)
Joan:	OK? Being better, making more A's, getting more degrees, doing better than this one, that one.
Stuart:	All of that is the excess of Controlling-Taking, your other main preference. It's an attempt at mastery, to prove that you are superior.
Larry:	You've done it already.
Stuart:	You've done it, long ago.
	(*How much is enough? Why isn't it satisfying?*)
Joan:	Yes, that's the thing. Why must I still prove it again and again and again?
Stuart:	Why is there that insatiable quality?
Joan:	Yes, it is insatiable, I will admit. There is a void that is never filled, Stuart.
	(*Maslow is right—D needs. Needs deprived early never seem filled.*)
Stuart:	You're not going to stop trying to prove that you're superior until you truly believe you're superior.
Joan:	No, I think I've reached that point of believing it. But I think the habit is so ingrained. I don't

feel . . . I feel I've proved the point already, but I feel it's non-productive for me to have proven that point. I need to go back and let in all the stuff I closed off somehow. I know I closed doors along the way, I deliberately closed doors. Now for instance, I went to college. OK, I chose the highly intellectual side of college life. And I let all those other girls go by me, all those guys, the ones that were playing bridge the whole day in the dorm, the ones that were fooling around, going to the pizza places. Joan was in the library. Joan was studying night and day. Joan was proving that she could be of the intellectual elite. OK?

(No wonder she's fascinated by Larry—his playing, his non-seriousness, the Larry-go-lightly side.)

Stuart: You were at a crossroads. You had to make a decision. To go into the library and to become intellectually superior, or to socialize. You made a choice.

Joan: I made a deliberate choice.

Stuart: What was the basis of the choice? Why did you choose that direction?

Joan: Well, a lot of things. First of all, the way I was brought up, my mother and father were not social beings. They were family beings. They were very close—talk about cubicles. Well, we had multiple cubicles, but the whole cubicle was encased. All right, my father had no outside interests at all, not at all. It was just building a business so his children would be fed, his children would have this and his wife would have that. Completely materialistic in orientation and family nurturing. Nurturing in the sense of providing food and shelter. But there was a basic lack of emotional nurturing there. There were too many children, I told you I was one of seven, OK? All the material things were there. The houses were there, we were all in the house, but I never felt I had enough love, enough touching, enough playing, I mean it was . . . we were not a happy close family, despite the seven children. We were close in terms of being crunched together in the houses.

(Never enough, so the insatiable quest started here.)

Stuart: Brothers and sisters?

Joan: Oh yes. Well, I passed them by long ago. Neither of my sisters went to college. All of my brothers went to college . . . I had a dreadful reaction to my mother, I think. Because my mother, even though she was fertile, and productive, and reproductive, she was, to me, not nurturing.

Stuart: Yes, that's very possible.

Joan: So I think I grew up with unfulfilled desire somehow.

Stuart: To be nurtured?

Joan: Insatiability. It was acquisition in a way, acquisition of intelligence, acquistion of things, mastery of tasks, proving points, you know, again and again.

(What a bottomless pit—deprivation.)

Stuart: In effect, you may have been saying, "See, mother, I am worthwhile after all. I'm worthy of being fed and nurtured."

Joan: Yes, but the nurturing . . . We always got too much feeding, you see, too much feeding and not nurturing. You know what I mean?

Stuart: Oh, exactly. You can stuff yourself and not feel nurtured.

Joan: OK, well that's it. You asked me why I was discontent. Well, I had everything, I have everything . . .

Stuart: But what you wanted.

Joan: It might stem from that. It's been difficult for me living with my mother these past weeks. Because to me, she had not accomplished anything, except breeding.

Stuart: Reproducing automatically.

Joan: Breeding, reproducing, and it's been very strange. I think a lot of tension that I've been undergoing, a lot of the emotional things that have been happening to me over this period of time, have to do with not only getting into myself once again through my writing but being pitted against another alternate lifestyle. I mean, I had long ago put all thoughts of my beginning away from me. I had pushed it away. My mother and father had such a lack of planning. I mean they were like will-o'-the-wisps.

(She took on Conserving-Holding because they didn't value it.)

Something would happen which would cause them to react. They would never plan ahead, make a thing happen or not happen. It would just happen, and they would deal with it as it happened. Whether it was insurance, buying things, selling things, or people getting hurt, or whatever it was, they just let fate take over.

(She wanted them to be more Controlling-Taking. That's her second orientation.)

Stuart: They were resigned. What will be, will be, and we'll deal with it.

Joan: I was very different from them, I mean, I don't know, it's hard to go back that far. This has forced me to think, you know, about my own work.

Larry: That's good.

Joan: Which I've got to do now. I've got to put it all together some way, and rationally.

(Yes, that's the Conserving-Holding way.)

Larry: I'll trade you spots. From all that he's saying, I think it's easier coming from where you're coming from than where I'm coming from.

(You do want structure, some system.)

Joan: Really? You think so? I don't know what's easier. Everyone has his own burden.

Stuart: Everyone has places in which they're stuck. We need to redirect our energy into the productive use of our strengths—by controlling our excesses. Ironically, we can get unstuck by using our strengths less, by supplementing ourselves with people who are different, who can be a check and balance on the excess, who can add new strengths to what we are doing, to get us unstuck. We need to extend ourselves by using our least preferred strengths more, so we can be our own check and balance, and get ourselves unstuck.

Joan: Yes, I have to think of it in those terms. I'm going to read further.

(Yes, the terms are important.)

Stuart: The traditional language of one's burden, sickness —I can't buy that. I've worked carefully to find a framework, language, phrases that will focus on what next step we need to take, how we need to redirect our energy by doing more of this and less of that. We need to think of the negative positively, balance right and wrong, good and bad, with more or less.

* * *

This transcript was from a day-long LIFO Training session, and though it was only one session, the participants covered crucial issues about their strengths and excesses that had gone unverbalized and unattended. You observed how the LIFO Strategies—Confirming, Capitalizing, Moderating, Supplementing, Extending and Bridging—added new dimensions to Joan and Larry's thinking. It also added new directions for improving their productivity and satisfaction.

The choice for improvement is theirs. LIFO Training presented them with the opportunity and the framework to exercise their options.

13

SUCCESS STRATEGIES

OPTIONS AT HOME AND WORK

Life is like a kaleidoscope. We are caught in its everchanging patterns, but we try to freeze a favorite pattern. We try to control and order life around us, and within us.

We look for structure, for patterns, something to organize the human experience, something to give us direction and guide the journey of our life.

Some structures are political or religious or economic, but the structure I am about to describe is humanistic. It is a personal structure that provides guidelines for making the most of our strengths and our personal energy at home and work. It follows six strategies.

First among the strategies is *Confirming*. This means identifying our game plan with its unique strengths. Confirming also means finding out what is right about us, who we are and what we prefer. This needs to be done, using a common language so that we can communicate our findings to one another.

Secondly, we need to put energy into *Capitalizing*. We need to make sure that other people know and respond consistently to our orientations and to our strengths as a person. Our work, our social and home life need to be checked out to see if our strengths are being appreciated and utilized.

A third strategy is *Moderating.* To avoid doing too much of a good thing, we need to gear back on our strengths. Curbing excess saves time and energy. It also helps avoid disruption in our key relationships.

Fourth is *Supplementing.* In planning and decision making, we need to find people who are different from us and whose perspective and strengths can be added to our own. This can uncover our blind spots and reduce the chance for major mistakes and lost opportunity.

Closely related to this is the fifth strategy of *Extending.* With this, we need to stretch ourselves just a bit. In case the people who supplement us are not available, we need to learn their perspectives and practice some of their strengths.

The final and sixth strategy is *Bridging.* We need to cross over into the world of other people's preferred orientations. We need to communicate with them in ways that are consistent with their orientations. It may create some discomfort for us at first, but the reward for the inconvenience is getting through to them more clearly and more quickly.

These are the success strategies—Confirming, Capitalizing, Moderating, Supplementing, Extending and Bridging. They have been described and illustrated throughout the previous chapters. Now I will summarize them to make them easier to apply.

CONFIRMING

No matter how successful we are, no matter how long we live, we need to confirm who we are and what is special about us. Confirmation is a life-long process, starting early in infancy. One of the difficulties in confirming ourselves is the lack of a common language to do so.

It is much easier to describe ourselves physically—tall or short, round-faced or brown-eyed. Another way to describe ourselves is by our work. If you ask people who they are they will say, "I'm a foreman, teacher, plumber, accountant, pilot or waitress." Seldom will people say something like, "I'm a person who likes to get things done quickly, and who likes pursuing many interests at once, rather than concentrating on one at a time."

People do not define themselves by their actions and strengths, only by occupations and their role as man, woman, father, daughter, husband, sister, teenager. And with these labels comes a variety of associations, assumptions, beliefs and stereotypes.

If a person has had serious personality problems, they will often define themselves—with the aid of professionals—by the label of their difficulty, "I'm an alcoholic, manic-depressive, paranoid, asthmatic, bedwetter." The language and labels of abnormality are plentiful. But where are the labels and language of normality to define and confirm ourselves?

With the Life Orientations model of human behavior, we have a language and a set of *normal* labels to classify, define, and give ourselves needed confirmation. The four orientations to life—Supporting-Giving, Controlling-Taking, Conserving-Holding and Adapting-Dealing—provide a way in which we can share and compare who we are and what is important to us. It helps us build and reinforce our personal identity. Our orientations, game plans and strengths describe us in ways that are useful for our satisfaction, communication and productivity.

The Life Orientations model is a language of normality. It is a classification system for normal people.

In our past, many of us have been confirmed with negative statements and labels—what's wrong with us. This led to feelings of inadequacy and ideas that we did not measure up. Some of our favorite negative labels are "dummy, jerk, stupid, idiot, weakling, slow poke, big mouth." What we needed was a large dose of "positive regard"—a reminder that we have strengths and value. Ironically, that is not easy to take.

In the early days of group dynamics, we had a group activity called The Strength Bombardment. People in a group would take turns allowing other group members to bombard them with positive statements about their strengths. The ground rule was that no one could make negative statements.

To speak only about a person's strengths was difficult for group members. It was equally difficult for the bombarded people to accept the positive regard. They would make disclaimers and give qualifications about their strengths. People would also laugh and be embarrassed by all the praise, but after a while, they became accustomed to it.

After being bathed in positive regard, and after receiving a massive dose of confirmation, the person would next hear about his or her weaknesses. However, they were not called weaknesses. The group stated them as "reservations" they had about the person's chances of fully using his or her strengths.

As a result of this experience, I placed Confirming as the first success strategy. I learned that before we try to help somebody or "set them straight," building appreciation is a prerequisite. This does not mean old-fashioned flattery, "buttering-up." It means genuine expressions of the strengths, first.

If we cannot think of another person's strengths, or if we say they do not have any, it usually indicates that the person's orientations are different from our own. The strengths have gone unnoticed. Sometimes we may have seen the strengths, but we focused exclusively on the excesses.

In some measure, we are continuously confirming ourselves. Whatever we do, and despite the satisfactions in the activity, the need for confirmation is always present. We want to be OK in our eyes and the eyes of other people.

The other part of Confirmation is the need to have a clear sense of who we are and what we stand for. Often that is easier to do by focusing on what we are not, how we are different from other people.

While on the one hand we like people who are similar to us—a reflected image of ourselves—we also utilize people who are different. They sharpen our picture of ourselves by the contrast.

With Life Orientations classifications, we have the opportunity to compare ourselves and focus on how we are the same and different. The act of classifying ourselves—what orientations we prefer most and least—serves the need for Confirmation.

It is the beginning. It is the basis for getting what we want and getting along. Growth and relationships depend on knowing ourselves, having a clear identity. That is why this book is called "The Name of Your Game." If, as a result of reading the book you only classify yourself and others, you have still accomplished an important strategy.

But before I go on to the next strategy, I have a recommendation. Bombard yourself. Make a list of all your strengths. Approach your boss, a co-worker, friends, your spouse or children. Ask them to tell you your strengths. It only "hurts" a little while. If you are brave, you will ask them to tell you what reservations they have about your fully using your strengths.

CAPITALIZING

After we have a positive way to describe our strengths, we need to determine how we can use them to the fullest. We need to find out what's best for us.

Each of us needs an opportunity to be ourselves and carry out our work and our lives in a way that is consistent with our game plan and our strengths.

If we prefer Supporting-Giving, what is best for us?

The most positive environment is:	*The most negative environment is:*
• Respecting	• Betrayal
• Encouraging	• Personal criticism
• Reassuring	• Ridicule
• Idealistic	• Lack of support

If we are Controlling-Taking, what is best for us is different.

The most positive environment is:	*The most negative environment is:*
• Competitive	• Resources restricted
• Risk-taking	• Authority countermanded
• Challenging	• Responsibility diminished
• Novel	• No challenges

For those of us whose game plan is Conserving-Holding,

The most positive environment is:	*The most negative environment is:*
• Unemotional	• Constant changes
• Factual	• Highly emotional
• Inquiring	• Premature decision-making
• Practical	• Failure to be taken seriously

Finally, if Adapting-Dealing is our preference, then,

The most positive environment is:	*The most negative environment is:*
• Social	• Unfriendly co-workers
• Flexible	• Critical authority
• Informal	• Routines and details
• Accepting	• Firm schedules and supervision

In some situations we may encounter conditions that are not consistent with our orientations. This can create considerable dissatisfaction and stress. As much as possible, we need to express our strengths. We need to arrange our life at home and work in ways that allow us to capitalize on our strengths and uniqueness.

MODERATING

Too much of a good thing can waste energy, lose time, and cost money. How much is just right? We usually know, because events flow smoothly and we accomplish what we want.

Too much is usually accompanied by tension and complaints from other people that we are overdoing things. In each of the case histories in this book, excess played a role in the difficulty. Stress and conflict led to excess. Excess added tension to an already stressful situation. Sometimes stress was self-induced and helped to create a stressful situation.

To moderate, we need to do less of, gear back, and find the appropriate level of effort. Remember, this does not mean we have to change ourselves. We have only to adjust the *amount* of whatever we are overdoing.

In moderating, we need the help of other people. Because it is easy to slip over into excess, we need other people to alert us when we do. By calling our attention to it early, we can reverse our direction with less strain on ourselves. Usually, we will have less attachment to our actions at the earlier stage and less need to save face, or justify ourselves.

With some self-awareness, we can begin to observe our

MODERATING TECHNIQUES FOR REVERSING EXCESS

ORIENTATION:	EXCESS CLUES:	MODERATING TECHNIQUES:	GIVE REASSURANCE THAT THEY ARE:
Supporting-Giving	• Apologetic remarks • May seem to decide, then back off • Overly critical or moralistic	• Provide support, reassurance and encouragement • Hear the other person out and offer help • Provide meaningful reasons for actions • Have patience with concerns	• Seen as responsible and worthwhile • Valued, understood, accepted, trusted • Idealistic, but not in vain
Controlling-Taking	• Gets defensive, argues, and tries to out-expert you • Wants it their way • Very impatient during explanations	• Ask questions to help person feel they can find their own solutions • Provide an alternative to view situation • Give people the feeling they are making the decision • Be open and firm, but respectful	• Capable and competent • Capable of overcoming obstacles • Able to capture opportunities
Conserving-Holding	• Attacks small points and logic—gets into "analysis-paralysis" • Overly silent or non-committal reactions • May put you off with request for more information	• Minimize emotions • Develop criteria to evaluate completeness and accuracy • Allow for some cool-off time or delay in decision making • Get some additional facts the person will trust	• Seen as objective, purposeful and rational • Safe and secure with few surprises to come • Not in a situation of overwhelming loss
Adapting-Dealing	• Kids around and doesn't get serious • Overly agreeable, yet stalls • May be willing to accept smaller plan just to placate you	• Reassure the person of likability • Use positive approach to objections: "What I like about your concern is . . ." • Be willing to try for compromise • Show how approval can be gained by making the decision	• Seen as likable and easy to get along with • Accepted because everyone is happy with the effort • Not locked in but have a chance for flexibility

own threshholds, what actions are the forerunners of our excess. These are early warning signs of excess. In the chapter on "Overplaying Our Game," I have listed certain intermediate actions between strength and excess. By studying those in your most preferred orientation, you will catch yourself earlier and moderate your strengths *before* they become excessive.

Often, however, we cannot catch ourselves and we slip into excess. It may run for some time without our knowledge. This is when we need trusted and respected people to hold the mirror up to us, so that we can see what we are doing. There are specific approaches that people can take with us, or that we can take alone in helping others to stop excess.

The accompanying table shows some techniques for reversing excess, for turning weaknesses back to strengths.

SUPPLEMENTING

As I have indicated previously, most of us do not have a full complement of strengths or total perspective. This comes about because we have one of the four orientations that ranks low on our list. This least preferred orientation can come back to us in unfavorable ways.

As I described in the chapter called "That's Not My Game," we can easily overlook opportunities or make major mistakes because of the blind spot created by our least preferred orientation. Without doubt, we can be more productive if we allow people with different strengths and perspectives to supplement us. Then we can play the game with a full deck, a complete complement of strengths from all four suits.

Most of us need to go "shopping" among our family members, co-workers, friends and bosses who are different from us to add to our supply of strengths. We must remember, however, if we liked the game plan from which these strengths are derived, we would have been using it.

So we need to take it a step at a time. We need to choose only a few strengths to add to our supply. In this way, we will not feel overwhelmed from trying out a full set of strengths from our least preferred orientation. Rather, we can slowly become accustomed to a few and increase the possibility that we will allow them to supplement us.

Here is a list of strengths from each orientation. Look them over and select one or two from your least preferred orientation that could increase your productivity. Take a strength supplement. Add to your effectiveness.

WHICH STRENGTHS WOULD YOU LIKE TO ADD?

SUPPORTING-GIVING STRENGTHS

- Keeping an eye on quality
- Being responsive to the needs of others
- Relating not to what is, but to what ought to be
- Focusing on what's best, fair and just for all

CONTROLLING-TAKING STRENGTHS

- Creating a sense of urgency to get things started
- Sensing opportunities and what's required to seize them
- Willing to confront and bargain hard for a fair share
- Organizing others and taking charge of uncertain situations

CONSERVING-HOLDING STRENGTHS

- Keeping a cool head in the midst of crisis
- Seeing the trade-offs in situations
- Making the most of what there is before going to the new
- Testing to make sure things work

ADAPTING-DEALING STRENGTHS

- Keeping in touch with people's thoughts and feelings
- Using the light touch and taking the strain out of serious situations
- Demonstrating flexibility and making workable compromises
- Adopting and facilitating the goals of others

Now that you have selected your strength supplement, think of someone who has those strengths. If you cannot think of anyone (because you haven't paid much attention to those kinds of people), then be more aware of the strengths you are shopping for, and you will soon find them.

When you do, ask that person to review your important plans, problems or decisions. You will hear questions and get answers that will uncover your blind spots.

EXTENDING

Suppose your supplementing person has no time, or just can't see you when you're available. Don't worry, you can learn to use that person's strengths and perspectives by yourself. Since you have watched the person as they supplemented you, you can try out their strengths on your own.

At first, select some low-risk situation, one that is not too important, since you will feel awkward using them. After a while, they can become as natural to use as your most preferred strengths.

You can learn to be more responsive to others, more assertive, more analytical or more harmonious. You can also learn to ask yourself the special questions of each orientation. If you do, you can make presentations, plans or decisions that have total perspective.

Be patient in your learning. Your least preferred game plan may have been infrequently used for considerable time. At some point in your life it could have been more useful to you, but circumstances may have shifted your preferences.

It is also likely that you decided not to pursue a set of strengths because it was not demonstrated with frequency in your background. No one may have been around who did things that way, so that you had no exposure to it, no model to follow.

There is another basis for the choice of our least preferred orientation. As we were growing up, some key person in our life may have been oriented that way. We noticed their progress in life and came to the conclusion that their lives were not advanced by their actions. If their orientation produced that unhappy result, certainly we would have no part of it. It did not work for them, and it probably would not work any better for us.

In many cases, there is another reason why the least preferred orientation becomes such a low priority. A key person raising us may have demonstrated considerable excess in that orientation. That excess became our definition of the orientation. With so much of the excess on our minds, we could not make room for the strengths—let alone appreciate them. Therefore we rejected the entire orientation and sometimes even the *people* who lived by it.

Previously, I described how I reacted to my mother's Conserving-Holding orientation. Mistakenly, I interpreted that orientation as being bothersome because of excessive need for predictability and information. I did not appreciate my mother's strengths of preserving what little we had when I was growing up, and doing wonders with our limited resources.

Another example will illustrate the virtual aversion we can have for our least preferred orientation. One colleague was very concerned that he would not be able to work with people who preferred Adapting-Dealing. He just shook his head in dismay. To him, those were unacceptable ways to conduct one's life.

He was doubly concerned because the following week he had to work with a group whose most important people preferred Adapting-Dealing. In a discussion with several other people, he was unable to isolate why he reacted to it so negatively.

As a part of the professional training in which he was participating, I paired him with another professional—a woman—whose most preferred orientation was Adapting-Dealing. They had to discuss and interpret each other's Life Orientations survey results—why they preferred their strengths and why they had value for them.

After one hour of discussion with her, he realized the reason behind his antipathy for Adapting-Dealing. It seems he and his brother were always at odds with their father. Influencing their father to get what they wanted was a constant struggle.

On the other hand, their younger sister never had a problem. As he described it, she had their father "eating out of her hand." She got everything she wanted. And she did it by winning their father over, being adaptable, flexible, joking, finessing him right out of his toughness. The boys went power against power. They thought her way was dishonest, shameful, a sell-out.

What amazed him about his discovery was that his discussion partner, whose preference was Adapting-Dealing, was quite a fine person. He found her professional, intelligent and helpful—not at all like his sister!

In your own case, think for a moment. What is the basis for your choice of your least preferred orientation? It helps to know. That information can smooth the way for Extending.

BRIDGING

For the most part, we live in our own world. We are alone with our private thoughts and feelings. When we are with other people, we feel connected by their presence, but we still have our private thoughts and feelings.

Love helps us cross over the bridge to the world of another. It provides the desire, the energy and pathway to understand and appreciate each other. Love can generate the need and desire to communicate. Work also creates the need and desire to communicate. We must accomplish with and through each other. We have practical reasons for getting along—there is a job to be done.

Whether at home or at work, our worlds can collide, particularly when our preferred orientations are opposite. When my *most* preferred way is your *least,* we have a long bridge to cross.

As I illustrated in the case of the Apologetic Executive and in the chapter on "Communication Gaps," there are special ways we want people to communicate with us. This depends in large measure upon our preferred orientations. When we are different, bridging does not come naturally. We have to make a conscious, if not self-conscious, effort to cross over into the other person's world, to approach them in ways that are understandable and meaningful to *them.*

Here is a reminder of how to enter the world of another person, to open their ears so that they can hear our information. Listed below are the recommended ways to communicate through each orientation. Whether we are parent and child, husband and wife, boss and subordinate, doctor and patient, two friends or two lovers, the ways to bridge are suggested below.

HOW TO BRIDGE TO EACH ORIENTATION

SUPPORTING-GIVING

- Ask for help
- Stress worthwhile causes
- Acknowledge trust
- Allow mutual goal setting

CONTROLLING-TAKING

- Offer opportunity
- Demonstrate competence
- Be responsive
- Spar on an equal basis
- Be direct

CONSERVING-HOLDING

- Be organized
- Tie new things to old
- Present ideas as low risk
- Give opportunity to be analytical
- Move ahead slowly

ADAPTING-DEALING

- Be friendly and informal
- Express intent and preference
- Let them know you are pleased
- Show flexibility
- Display sense of humor

Now you may say, "Why should I do all the work? Why can't they cross over to my world, or at least meet me halfway across the bridge?"

Well, for one thing, we have no control over the other person. We could insist or demand that they be more like us, but that is likely to encourage defensiveness and communications that miss their mark. Whether we like it or not, we have the intial responsibility for getting across to another person. If we want to accomplish what we have set out to do—and we must do it with or through the other person—then the burden of initiative is with us.

This, however, does not mean we have to become similar

to the other person, give up our own preferences and identity. It means merely that we manage our information and present it first in the other person's terms. That is editorializing a communication. It is not major surgery on one's personality.

Ideally, the other person might meet us halfway. Ultimately they may, but someone has to go first. When we do start across the bridge, the other person often makes a step in our direction. But we will never know, if we do not take the first step. It is surprising how many relationships reverse, not only improve, when one party takes the initiative. But there are times, of course, when the bridge is long and the journey weary and hazardous.

Then, again, all bridges look long from our side. To break the illusion, we need to start out on the trip to get a better idea of the extent of the crossing.

Those are the Success Strategies—Confirming, Capitalizing, Moderating, Supplementing, Extending and Bridging. Those are some options for greater success at home and at work. They provide unlimited possibilities for expanding our game plan, seeing new opportunities and solving old problems.

14

FROM FREUD
TO ROGERS
TO MASLOW

THE ORIGINS AND THEORETICAL
BACKGROUND OF LIFE ORIENTATIONS®
THEORY AND TRAINING

Life Orientations Training is an applied behavioral science system which fosters individual and organizational productivity. It starts by having individuals, pairs, or groups identify their basic orientations to life. These are called Supporting-Giving, Controlling-Taking, Conserving-Holding, and Adapting-Dealing.

With the orientations as reference points, six LIFO strategies for growth and greater productivity are suggested. These are called Confirming, Capitalizing, Moderating, Bridging, Supplementing and Extending.

Underlying the Training is Life Orientations® theory. It has its roots in psychoanalysis, self-actualization theory, client-centered therapy, and group dynamics. Though the origins are eclectic, their final synthesis in LIFO Training has blended smoothly as it has evolved over a twenty-year period from my personal and professional experiences.

In a sense, Life Orientations Theory started with Freud. His concepts of psycho-sexual development and of character structure are the major source of the behavioral descriptions in the Training. Freud's early labels for the psycho-sexual stages of development were oral, anal, and phallic. Development, however, could be arrested at any level. He called this fixation.

In Life Orientations Theory, the oral orientation is Supporting-Giving, the phallic is Controlling-Taking, and the anal is Conserving-Holding. A fourth orientation is called Adapting-Dealing and has no counterpart in psychoanalysis. The orientations in Life Orientations Theory are viewed as *givens and choices after childhood,* not as fixated character structure.

In Freud's early theorizing about developmental stages, he also suggested some character traits. But he had no theory of *generalized forms of stable functioning* or of consistent patterning. Freud, in 1908, and his followers Ernest Jones, in 1918, and Karl Abraham, in 1921, wrote papers that touched secondarily on character.[1] Their concerns were pathology, symptom formation, and the "choice of neurosis" as it relates to being fixated at a particular level of psycho-sexual development.

Wilhelm Reich, in 1933, first used the concept of character to describe general and stabilized ways of functioning.[2] But while his focus was on character as a total formation, it was as a neurotic solution to infantile, instinctual conflict around the instinctual drives of sex and aggression. Unlike Freud, Jones and Abraham, Reich did not see character as a defensive way of combating infantile conflict. But when these defenses ultimately crystallized and became hardened and detached from their origins, and became independent of their original instinctual drives and conflicts, then that was termed "character." Character, as defined by Reich, was an attempt at mastery over the conflicts and impulses, and character bound the impulses in a stable way. This he called "character armor."

In Life Orientations Theory, the orientations to life (character orientations) are also viewed as generalized and stable forms of functioning that have autonomy and independence from their early source. However, the orientations are not viewed as defenses, hardened and neurotic, but as modes, first of a productive, fully functioning person. Secondly, these orientations can be productive modes

---

1   Freud, Sigmund: *"Character and Anal Eroticism" 1908,* Collected Papers *Vol. II, pp. 45-50, Basic Books, New York, 1959. Ernest Jones: "Anal Character Traits" 1918,* Papers on Psychoanalysis, *pp. 531-555, William Wood, Baltimore, 1938. Karl Abraham: "Contributions to the Theory of Anal Character" 1921,* Selected Papers on Psychoanalysis, *pp. 370-392, Basic Books, New York, 1957.*

2   Reich, Wilhelm: Character Analysis 1933, *p. 144, Orgone Institute Press, New York, 1949.*

to handle defensive conditions stimulated by the external world. They become unproductive as defenses only when they are used to excess.

If the unproductive excessive behavior has greater frequency than the fully functioning, productive behavior, then it can be said that the person is using his or her orientations in a "neurotic," defensive way. If a person has continually responded in the unproductive excessive mode, so that it has become habitualized, even though there is no longer a real threat in the environment, then "character armor" is a distinct possibility, and it may represent total functioning.

Like Reich's theory, Life Orientations theory formulates character orientations as general forms of functioning with a stable existence. Unlike his, my theory holds that orientations have a productive, independent function, and are *not* used solely for defensive purposes.

Many years after Reich's contribution, Erich Fromm, in 1947, and Erik H. Erikson, in 1950, added new dimensions to character orientations and character development.[3] Fromm blended his theory of character orientations with a more modern concept of people having both productive and unproductive behavior.

Following a different path, Erikson illustrated in detail how character orientations are general forms of functioning, and he formulated a theory outlining the progressive steps in the development of character.

Erikson, along with his new formulations of the pscho-sexual stages of development, added the child's pscyho-motor development as a parallel and intertwined process. A developmental phase was no longer a matter of the random fate of the instinct, but was focused into social ways of functioning, a frame of mind and an attitude.

In fact, Erikson extended the physiological and psycho-sexual development of the child into a series of psycho-social crises.[4] For example, the oral phase of development which is generated by sensory-kinesthetic development focuses the feeding-feeling child on "to get, to

---

3   Fromm, Erich: Man For Himself, *Fawcett Publications, Greenwich, Conn., 1947. Erikson, Erik:* Childhood and Society, *Norton, New York, 1950.*

4   *Erikson, Erik: "Identity and the Life Cycle,"* Psychological Issues, *Vol. 1, No. 1, International Universities Press, New York, 1959.*

give in return," which then leads to the psycho-social crisis of developing *trust versus mistrust.*

The anal phase follows muscular development which then centers the child "to hold on or to let go," which in turn fosters a psycho-social crisis around developing *autonomy versus shame and doubt.*

In the third traditional psycho-analytic phallic stage of development, Erikson added the implication of new skills in locomotion, "to go after things and intrude." The psycho-social crisis at this stage is the development of *initiative versus guilt.*

Going beyond the tradition of psychoanalysis, Erikson extended the study of human development past childhood through adulthood. He also broke with the absolute idea of fixation—getting stuck in one psycho-sexual stage. He believed that there could be unresolved psycho-social issues at any level, but a person would not necessarily be fixated at that level. Satisfactory development at the next stage was possible.

Going further, Erikson says that development does not stop at childhood as Freud and his early followers formulated. Erikson adds four stages of *adult* growth with their parallel social crisis. The stages are *identity* (to be oneself and to share it) versus *diffusion* (not to be oneself), *intimacy* (to lose and find oneself in another) versus *isolation* (to withdraw from another), *generativity* (to make be and to take care of) versus *self-absorption* (strive for more), *integrity* (to be through having been and to face not being) versus *despair* (running from facing not being).

Though the four orientations to life in Life Orientations theory reflect Erikson's social implications of orientations, they are conceptualized as adult choices. The choices are made after experiencing the orientations in earlier psycho-sexual stages of childhood.

In Life Orientations theory, Supporting-Giving (oral), Conserving-Holding (anal), and Controlling-Taking (phallic) are seen as generalized stable forms of functioning, and as optional ways of successfully coping, free from "instinctual," "conflicting," "neurotic," or "armored" origins in childhood, similar to the psycho-analysts who emphasized ego psychology.[5] Orientations are viable psycho-social *choices* to

5 Hartmann, Heinz: Ego Psychology and the Problem of Adaptation, *International Universities Press, New York, 1958.*

cope with the *adult* world.

Life Orientations Training makes possible the identification of these choices, their psycho-social value, and their negative consequences. Furthermore, the Training makes available learning opportunities to experience the values of all orientations, and makes it possible to incorporate all three modes of functioning into one's own psycho-social repertoire. As a result, people can better cope and understand the personal and social trade-offs of each orientation and the mutual impact of different or similar orientations on a relationship.

Following Erikson's extension of character development into all ages of adult life, Life Orientations theory also outlines the differences at each stage of adult development according to an individual's choice of orientations. Adults go through the life cycle facing the same psycho-social issues at every stage, but there are distinct individual differences that stem from their choice of orientations.

For example, all psycho-social issues such as trust, autonomy, initiative, intimacy, generativity, integrity, are not the monopoly of any stage of character development. They are, in fact, *characteristically influenced* by the choice of orientations. There are four unique ways to manifest trust, autonomy, initiative, and so forth, depending upon which character orientation one chooses and favors.

Erich Fromm, on the other hand, in conceptualizing character orientations and their development, remained close to Freud.[6] But as a sociologist, psychoanalyst, and social philosopher, Fromm added two important new elements—the marketing orientation and the concept of productive and unproductive orientations. He was able to add these dimensions because he saw a limitation in Freud's belief that character traits were the result of various forms of instinctual drive diverted into sublimation or converted into reaction formation. Following Harry Stack Sullivan's neo-Freudian emphasis on interpersonal relationships,[7] Fromm relates development of character orientations to an individual's *relatedness* to others, to nature, to society and to oneself—not to sexual energy, as described in Freud's libido theory.

---

6   Fromm, Erich, op. cit. pp. 47-122.

7   Sullivan, Harry Stack: The Interpersonal Theory of Psychology, *Norton, New York, 1953.*

But Fromm still follows Freud in believing that character traits are not behavior traits. Character traits *underlie* outward behavior and must be inferred from the outer behavior. The character traits are a powerful force influencing behavior, and the basic entity in character is not a particular trait but a total organization. He called it "orientation of character." This orientation of character develops from two specific kinds of *relatedness* to the world: acquiring and assimilating *things,* and reacting to *people.* The former he calls assimilation and the latter socialization.

Orientations, then, are the ways the individual relates to the world, and they constitute the core of character. Character, defined by Fromm, is the relatively permanent form in which human energy is canalized in the process of assimilation and socialization. Fromm considers these character systems—orientations—the human substitute for instincts in animals.

With assimilation and socialization as the two factors in the development of orientations, Fromm describes four types of character. He designates them as "unproductive orientations" and calls them the Receptive orientation, the Exploitative orientation, the Hoarding orientation, and the Marketing orientation.

In his descriptions and labels of these unproductive orientations, there is an extremely negative view. In Life Orientations theory, the unproductive aspects of orientations are called excesses. There are no designations for a separate *unproductive* orientation, but there is only the excess of a *unitary* orientation, having both productive (strengths) and unproductive (excess) aspects. Though Fromm finally accedes to the position that unproductive orientations can have positive aspects, these positive parts only exist to the degree the person has generated what Fromm calls a *productive orientation.* This is a superordinate orientation which regulates the other four unproductive ones.

As Fromm's labels suggest (except Marketing), the orientation descriptions are psychoanalytic and pessimistic. Receptive is the oral, passive character; Exploitative is the phallic, aggressive character; Hoarding is the anal-retentive character.

The Marketing orientation, Fromm explains, is a phenomenon of the modern era resulting from economic functions in modern society. Exchange value of commodities is related to people who are now seen as commodities connected to supply and demand. In this orientation, personality plays a predominant role, and "putting one's self across" and being saleable is paramount. If people experience themselves as a commodity, or their value is related to personal acceptance by those who need their services or who employ them, then they have a marketing orientation.

Fromm's model is illuminating, but it is complex, and at times confusing. By describing four unproductive character systems as both negative and positive, regulated by an overall, general orientation called Productive, he establishes the Productive orientation as an ideal model. This places the other unproductive orientations in an inferior position, making personal identification with them difficult.

From an applied behavioral science viewpoint, this is, generally, a negative model with negative language. This would not lend itself to public application or public acceptance. Fromm's labels and the psychoanalytic language are burdened with judgment and the inadequacy of everyone but the scientist. As a social commentary, or a fresh discourse on character, it makes an inestimable contribution. But the nature of the model makes its transfer to human performance in everyday life unlikely.

One other limitation occurs around Fromm's formulation of the marketing orientation. Something of Fromm's European background comes through in his description of the absurd outcome of commercialization on the human being. In the marketing orientation, there is the taint of the "Ugly American" and the "Death of a Salesman."

From fifteen years' experience with Life Orientations Training, and from the statistical information from the Life Orientations survey,[8] the marketing orientation as a preferred character system appears far less frequently in our sample than the other three orientations. This is not to imply that this orientation is not essential. But, clearly, the marketing orientation (modified and called Adapting-Dealing) is this country's least preferred orientation. In the past fifteen years, the only occasion that the Adapting-Dealing orientation appeared as a predominant one was when I conducted a

---

8 *Atkins, Stuart:* LIFO® Training Manual, *Stuart Atkins, Inc., Beverly Hills, 1980.*

seminar in the state of Wyoming. This was for professionals of both sexes representing many different health disciplines.

Unlike the general adult population,[9] school children in the fifth and sixth grades strongly prefer the Adapting-Dealing orientation.[10] In sharp distinction to Erich Fromm's interpretation of the behavior in the "marketing" orientation, the position of Life Orientations theory is that this orientation has a lot less to do with the socio-economic values of the modern era, being saleable and exercising one's exchange value as a commodity, and more to do with *pleasing and making oneself adaptable* to fulfill one's needs—as children must do when they are young and in the process of socialization with their parents and older siblings.

Finally, Fromm's concept of Productivity and the Productive orientation must be examined. He indicates that Freud and his followers gave a detailed analysis of the neurotic character, known also as the pre-genital character. What was missing, says Fromm, was the character of the "normal," "mature," "healthy" personality. Though Freud wrote about the Genital character (his mature, healthy model of a person), it was vaguely developed. It was described as a character structure of a person in whom the oral and anal sexual energy (the libido) had been subordinated to the dominance of genital sexuality. Maturity was then judged completed when there was a satisfactory sexual relationship with the opposite sex, and when someone was functioning well in the sexual *and* social spheres of life.

In contrast to Freud, "productiveness," explains Fromm, "is man's ability to use his powers and to realize the potentialities inherent in him." This foreshadowed Abraham Maslow's concept of self-actualization.[11]

In Fromm's definition, he emphasizes man's freedom to experience himself as the embodiment of his powers, that he is the actor and feels at one with them, not masked or alienated from them. This was more fully developed in his book, "Escape from Freedom."[12] It would be difficult, in Fromm's terms, if not impossible, to have a productive character in a totalitarian state dominated by an authoritarian

9   *Atkins, Stuart: Ibid.*

10 *Life Orientations® Training for Children, report of two Training workshops for children, LIFO Division, Stuart Atkins, Inc.*

11 *Maslow, Abraham:* Motivation and Personality, *Harper & Row, New York, 1970.*

12 *Fromm, Erich:* Escape from Freedom, *Farrar & Reinhart, New York, 1941.*

character. Man must be free, and not be dependent on someone who controls his powers.

His definition of productive, Fromm adds, is not to be confused with being able to produce something as would an artist or artisan. No product need be involved. Nor does it mean being an active person. There can be non-productive activity. It does mean the full use of power and potentialities, using one's full capacity. Full use of power does not mean to exert power *over* or to dominate others. Productiveness, in his definition, is an attitude, a way of being *related* to the world.

There are two ways to relate to the world, *reproductively* and *generatively*. Relating reproductively means to reproduce reality as it is, like a film making a literal record of it. Relating generatively means enlivening reality by re-creating it spontaneously through one's own reason and power. Sanity is also related to the balance between these two modes, as well as productiveness.

Productiveness is the something new that emerges as these two poles of reproductivity and generativity dynamically interact. The productive orientation, Fromm believes, *can* be involved in producing products, systems of thought, works of art, and material things, but the most important object of the productive orientation is man himself.

So it is with this kind of productiveness, the full use of potentiality, power, and reality that controls the various unproductive character orientations—the receptive, exploitative, hoarding, and marketing. The amount of productive orientation present determines to what degree the unproductive orientations will be used positively or negatively.

In Life Orientations theory, productiveness is viewed differently. All four orientations can be used productively or unproductively. There is no superordinate orientation acting as a regulator over the unproductive orientations. And, in Life Orientations Training, people are given guidelines to insure the full use of the power and potential inherent in any of the four orientations.

Productivity, in Life Orientations terms, is defined as the full use of one's own strengths and uniqueness *in relation to* the full use of the strengths and uniqueness of others. Being productive or unproductive can occur under three separate conditions—favorable, conflict, or stress. When the strength and uniqueness of all are being acknowledged, when people's differences and similarities are being managed to reach a common goal, it can be said that an individual, pair, or a group is productive.

In less philosophic terms, in the language of daily life, Life Orientations Training attacks the five enemies of human productivity:

FIVE BLOCKS TO FULL USE OF POWER AND POTENTIALITY

1. *WASTED EFFORT* from overdoing tasks and assignments, and doing what is not necessary.
2. *MAJOR MISTAKES* caused by missing information and limited perspective on plans and decisions.
3. *LOST OPPORTUNITY* when available options are screened out by blind spots.
4. *UNRESOLVED DIFFERENCES* in key relationships creating continuous competition over whose way is the better way.
5. *EXCESSIVE STRESS* which wears down vitality and alienates people from their power and from each other.

If people are to have the energy to build a "productive orientation," in Fromm's terms, or to "self-actualize" themselves, in Maslow's terms, then they must cope with these less philosophical and more applied problems. This is the mission of LIFO Training, to encourage progressive mastery over the five blocks to human productivity and self-actualization.

Life Orientations Training accomplishes this by helping people identify, understand, appreciate, and fully utilize their character orientations. And to complete human "relatedness," people also learn to enable others to express *their* uniqueness and learn to develop interpersonal skills and strategies to accomplish this. If this is accomplished, people will be related, and in Fromm's view, they will overcome a major obstacle in human existence—*maintaining the use of power and individuality, while being closely related to others.*

In 1954, seven years after Erich Fromm published his ideas on productivity and suggested the need for studying the healthy person, Abraham Maslow developed his concepts of self-actualization. He also "studied" the healthy, normal personality as an antidote to the emphasis of pathology in psychoanalysis.[13] His concept of self-actualization parallels the concept of the fully functioning personality conceived by Carl Rogers.[14] In Maslow's framework, however, he makes room for the unproductive aspects of his self-actualized people. He reports that they experience anxiety and guilt, and can be ruthless in pursuing their mission and purpose. Unlike Rogers, Maslow believes that the productive person is not perfect. But there is no theory to tie in those unproductive aspects to the productive side.

Though Maslow selects out-of-the-ordinary people as examples of healthy, self-actualized personalities—Abraham Lincoln, Albert Einstein, Eleanor Roosevelt, William James, to name a few—he believes that the ordinary person can self-actualize and realize their full capacities.

These capacities need only be liberated by filling basic needs which are in a hierarchy. The highest need in the hierarchy is self-actualization. But lower in the hierarchy, and in ascending order, are physiological needs, safety needs, belonging needs, and esteem needs. Since these needs must be fulfilled from lower to higher, human productivity, or self-actualization, has to wait its turn at the top of the need pyramid.

In Life Orientations Training, *all* the needs are being filled *simultaneously*. Built into the process and structure of the Training is a telescoping effect which compresses the hierarchy at every stage of the training, *and* concurrently engages the process of self-actualization.

Further, Life Orientations Training fills Maslow's criteria for the eight ways people can self-actualize:[15]

1. To become more aware of what is going on around, between, and within people.

2. To see life as a process of choices having positive and negative aspects, but to choose for growth even though there are risks.

---

13   *Maslow Abraham:* Motivation and Personality, *op. cit. pp. 149-202*

14   *Rogers, Carl:* Psychology: A Study of a Science, Vol. 3, Formulations of the Person and the Social Context, *Koch, Sigmond ed., McGraw Hill, 1959.*

15   *Maslow, Abraham:* The Far Reaches of Human Nature, *Viking Press, New York, 1971.*

3. To get in touch with the core and essential inner nature of ourselves including our values, tastes, and temperament.

4. To be honest about our needs and actions and take responsibility for them.

5. To learn to trust our judgment about ourselves and our needs so that we can make better life choices.

6. To continually develop our potentialities and see self-actualization not as an end-state, but as a never-ending process.

7. To have more peak experiences in which we are more aware, think, feel, and act more clearly and accurately.

8. To recognize our defenses and the way we distort our self-image and the image of the external world, and to work to remove these defenses.

It is interesting to note that Maslow's eight paths to self-actualization fill Fromm's two criteria for developing a productive orientation—relating to the world reproductively (recording reality more as it is) and generatively (putting one's own mark on reality by re-creating it through one's own uniqueness).

In Life Orientations theory, a major concept relating to productivity and self-actualization is excess. The psychology of excess dates as far back as the 5th Century B.C., when Lao Tzu[16] stated that "if you over-sharpen the blade, the edge will soon blunt." He also wrote that "the wise man is sharp but not cutting, pointed but not piercing, straightforward but not unrestrained, and brilliant but not blinding." And in the summary wisdom of Lao Tzu, "More is less and less is more."

William James also identified the human problem of excess and its effect on productivity.[17] He called it the "errors of excess." Love when excessive becomes possessiveness, an excess of loyalty becomes fanaticism. Any virtue can "diminish" the person when it is allowed to be expressed in its extreme form.

These errors of excess come from a certain blindness, according to James. This blindness, or lack of awareness, expresses itself in relationships, particularly in our inability to

---

16 Lao Tzu, (Translated by D.C. Lau): Tao Te Ching, Penguin, New York, 1964.

17 James, William: Talks to Teachers on Psychology and to Students on Life's Ideals, 1899, Henry Holt & Co., Dover, New York, 1950.

understand one another. If we are presumptuous and try to decide for others what is good for them, what their needs are, or what they should be taught, then we fall into error. Our failure to be aware of our blindness with one another, James contends, is a major source of our unhappiness with one another.

In Life Orientations Training, a major growth strategy called Bridging helps us recognize and overcome our "blindness" to the differences in the needs and values of others. It also helps us better understand the "inner reality" of other people and helps us stop presuming that we know what is good for others and what their needs are.

However, in Life Orientations theory, excess does not stem from this blindness we have with one another. Rather, it is a consequence of self-reinforcement when we derive pleasure from the use of our orientations and their strengths. When we over-do things, when we exaggerate our virtues, it is often for our own self-satisfaction.

Another source of excess in Life Orientations theory is unresolved stress. When threats to our needs are perceived, or when we are blocked from using our own preferred orientations, we experience stress. If we are unable to cope with these threats or to fill our needs, then, as Hans Selye says, we experience distress.[18] This is when we over-react with our strengths and virtues and become excessive.

Life Orientations Training also follows Carl Rogers' client-centered perspective and theory of therapy.[19] In seeking self-actualization and behavioral change in clients, the Training places the responsibility and control for growth in the hands of the client. The professional acts in the role of guide and clarifier as the client-learner follows the structure and sequence of the Training process.

Though there are a series of cognitive and structured exercises as stimuli, the rate of revelation and the depth of insight are controlled by the client. *Clients are in charge of their own analysis, interpretation, and learning within the given framework of the four orientations to life and the six strategies for growth.*

The Training starts with another Rogerian concept, "unconditional positive regard" for the client. By focusing on

---

18   Selye, Hans: Stress without Distress, *Lippincott, Philadelphia, 1974.*

19   Rogers, Carl: Client-Centered Therapy, *Houghton Mifflin, New York, 1951.*

the client's strengths and productive functioning, self-acceptance is generated as the forerunner for change. The Life Orientations concepts, the materials, and the Trainer withhold judgment and evaluation of the client, and the client can then experience unconditional positive regard.

In outlining the helping process and the helping relationship, Rogers provides clarity and form for the integration of all kinds of helping.[20] Life Orientations Training follows these steps in the helping relationship as outlined by Rogers:

1. The situation is defined.
2. There is encouragement of free expression.
3. The trainer accepts and clarifies.
4. There is expression of positive feelings.
5. There is a recognition of positive impulses for growth.
6. Insight develops.
7. Choices are clarified.
8. Positive action is generated.
9. More insight develops.
10. Increased autonomy.

Many of the concepts of Rogers and Maslow have found wide acceptance in the field of education and business and industry. Their positive view of human functioning, their ego-enhancing language, their emphasis on growth and the helping relationship, rather than on pathology, have made them major contributors to the field of applied behavioral science. Rogers became an encounter group therapist and practitioner.[21] Much of his theory and practice about group growth and functioning were applications of his theories on individual personality and growth.

In 1962, Maslow was sponsored by Andrew Kay, Owner and President of Non-Linear Systems, an electronics firm in Southern California. Kay, after attending a National Training Laboratories program for company presidents, offered his company as a laboratory to "test" the theories of leading scientists from universities across the country. Maslow's concepts were being applied in the group dynamics movement at the National Training Laboratories where Kay learned of

20 Rogers, Carl: Counseling and Psychotherapy, p. 30-44, Houghton Mifflin, New York, 1942.
21 Rogers, Carl: Carl Rogers on Encounter Groups, Harper & Row, New York, 1970.

Maslow. Kay sponsored Maslow's time to write "Toward a Psychology of Being."[22] During the summer of 1963, Maslow visited Non-Linear Systems again. He wanted to apply his theories of a healthy, self-actualized person to an organization. The result was his book, "Eupsychian Management."[23]

On a personal note, Andrew Kay was my client in 1960, when my field of specialization as a consultant was individual counseling and psychological testing. My interest in group dynamics was heightened by the behavioral science activity going on at Non-Linear. One of the behavioral scientists consulting with the company was James V. Clark from UCLA. In 1964, he invited me to become one of seven professionals he had chosen from across the country to participate in the first T-group intern program on the West Coast, sponsored by UCLA and the National Training Laboratories. Andrew Kay provided four separate working units of his company in which the interns could apply their newly learned group skills.

In T-groups, unlike individual counseling, there were no closed sessions. If anything was worth discussing, the norm was to disclose it in the group. All were privileged to the same information simultaneously. And it was possible to solve problems with all the parties present, rather than relying on random transfer of learning from a series of individual sessions.

During a luncheon discussion with Maslow, I mentioned my reluctance to write up my exciting new experiences in group work. My interest was not research. It was in recounting the unusual events of the group experience. Maslow encouraged me to write such an article because the events illustrated peak experiences. The scientific value of this, he pointed out, was that peak experiences could lead the way for relevant research.

From these experiences, and from publishing the article,[24] I became an associate of the NTL Institute of Applied Behavioral Science, and I traveled throughout the United States conducting T-groups and programs in human relations and group dynamics. The theoretical and applied framework

---

22   *Maslow, Abraham:* Toward a Psychology of Being, *Van Nostrand, N.J., 1962.*

23   *Maslow, Abraham:* Eupsychian Management, *Irwin, Illinois, 1965.*

24   *Atkins, Stuart and Kuriloff, Arthur H.: "T-Group for a Work Team,"* Journal of Applied Behavioral Science, *Vol. 2, No. 1, pp. 63-93, 1966.*

of the T-group and Laboratory Method was striking and hardhitting. It was engaging, encountering, and required an extended awareness in order to attend to the dynamics of a group and to the interaction of fifteen people instead of one.

T-groups (T for training) and the Laboratory method derived their impetus from the work of Kurt Lewin.[25] He developed a new language and model for describing the cause of individual behavior at a certain moment in time in a social context. He called it "life space." He emphasized the importance of painstaking observation of natural events and the present moment, the here and now. Recognizing the interdependence of all parts of an event, Lewin believed that behavioral scientists should not concentrate independently on cognition, learning, motivation, personality, and social influence, or culture. Behavior should be viewed from the standpoint of the *interaction* of the parts as a whole, with causation viewed as *contemporary* to the events, happening in the present and not, as in psychoanalysis, happening from the forces in the past.[26]

Lewin's investigations led him to the study of reward and punishment, conflict, and how these were induced by other people. In turn, that focused his interest on how one person, a group leader, for instance, could induce forces on a person to either help or restrict. In comparing his experiences in Germany with those in the United States, he was struck by the differences in leadership and the social-emotional atmosphere of groups. What followed was his classic study, in 1939, of types of leadership and of social atmospheres.[27]

Authoritarian, democratic, and laissez-faire leadership types and their induced social climates and group behaviors became a central focus in education, industry, health sciences, and government. It made an impact on the styles of managing, teaching, and helping people. Managers, teachers, therapists, nurses, doctors, social workers, and community workers were all examined and evaluated for their ability to be democratic, the ideal model of leader and member behavior.

Workshops were established to train leaders in democratic principles and practices. One such workshop took

---

25 Lewin, Kurt: Principles of Topological Psychology, McGraw Hill, New York, 1936.

26 Lewin, Kurt: A Dynamic Theory of Personality, McGraw Hill, New York, 1935.

27 Lewin, Kurt; Lippitt, Ronald; White, Robert: Patterns of Aggression in Experimentally Created Social Climates, Journal of Social Psychology, 1939, pp. 271-279.

place at the State Teachers College in New Britain, Connecticut in the summer of 1946.[28] The goal was to develop more effective local leaders in facilitating the understanding of, and compliance with, the Fair Employment Practices Act. Kurt Lewin and Ronald Lippitt headed the research team from the Research Center for Group Dynamics, then located at Massachusetts Institute of Technology. The training leaders were Kenneth D. Benne from Columbia University and Leland P. Bradford of the National Education Association, as well as Ronald Lippitt, who had a dual role as trainer and researcher.

Discussion was the principal methodology of the workshop, with some role-playing to diagnose problems and practice new approaches. Researchers were attached to the three learning groups to study the behavioral interactions of the participants. Early in the workshop, Kurt Lewin arranged evening meetings for the training staff and research team to review their observations of what was happening in the three groups. This included analysis and interpretation of leader, member, and overall group behavior.

Some participants asked to join these evening meetings, and the impact of hearing the descriptions and analysis of their behavior was astonishing. This confirmed Lewin's theory of the power in the moment. Discussions in the evenings around these process observations of the "here-and-now" behavior created a secondary evening workshop. The training staff realized that this procedure was powerful and that a process of re-education had been discovered inadvertently.

Kurt Lewin died in early 1947, but the training staff of the leadership workshop planned and implemented another workshop in Bethel, Maine in the summer of 1947. The workshop was content-laden with discussions around the most effective agenda for such workshops. Five small, ongoing groups were formed which were called BST groups (Basic Skills Training).

Because the workshop participants represented such a variety of occupations and professional disciplines, some common denominator needed to be identified to focus and integrate their learning. The workshop faculty designated the heterogeneous participants as "change agents." The Basic Skills Training groups, then, were ideal for training

28   Bradford, Leland P.; Gibb, Jack R.; Benne, Kenneth D.: T-Group Theory and Laboratory Methods, *John Wiley & Sons, Inc., New York, 1964.*

participants in the skills of human relations to be better change agents. They would be responsible for democratically inducing individual and social change in their back-home organizations.

By 1949, the NTL staff determined that the agenda of the BST group was overloaded by trying to juggle specific content *and* here-and-now process observations. The process observations were meant to foster group functioning and to advance the content learning. But it proved to be too much. (Content versus process became, and still is, a crucial variable in designing learning experiences.)

In 1949 and 1950, because of the intentional diversity of the new NTL staff, a shift took place in the nature of the program. The training content—what change agents needed to know and do to impact large social institutions—refocused to process observations of personal, interpersonal, and small-group behavior. This new process removed all formal content. Now, the group's agenda was to study itself, its members, its leaders, and their *interaction.*

The Lewinian and sociological emphasis became secondary in importance to the language and concepts of psychoanalysis and the client-centered theory of Carl Rogers. Along with this changing emphasis, the "BST" designation was dropped in favor of just "T-Groups."

Studying change and democratic values was still a major goal of the T-group and of the training laboratory. But the main activity became the exploration of the helping relationship.

The goal in training was the *prevention* of human difficulty through the development of "normal" people. Many diverse professionals in the helping fields were attracted to NTL and the T-group and Laboratory method. They were a crusading force in focusing other professionals toward helping "normal" people understand themselves and others better to solve individual and group problems. Their hope was that help would come *before* behavior became "abnormal," before there was a need to seek professional help. Maslow's self-actualization theory and emphasis on healthy personalities became a supportive force in NTL's quiet crusade.

At UCLA, in the late '50's and through the '60's, the Institute of Industrial Relations sponsored a West Coast version of the T-group, called Sensitivity Training. Their approach no longer centered on improving group functioning, the development of interpersonal skills, or the intellectual discussion of human relations problems. They were interested in "the total enhancement of the individual and the unfolding of a fully functioning personality."[29]

This meant helping individuals to experience people and events more fully, to know themselves more intimately and accurately, to find more meaning in life, and to be committed to growth and to ever-increasing personal power. Studying the desire to control others and be controlled, to manage love and anger, and to overcome loneliness, were also essential elements of Sensitivity Training.

Whether intentional or not, these purposes were consistent with Carl Rogers' theories and Erich Fromm's view of human productivity. Further, Sensitivity Training and T-groups were devoted to the development of theories and methodologies to *apply* the behavioral sciences to individuals, pairs, or groups. As a result, the National Training Laboratories changed its name to the NTL Institute for Applied Behavioral Science.

As a T-group trainer for NTL and a sensitivity trainer at UCLA from 1965 to 1972, I experienced the theory and practice of both T-groups and Sensitivity Training. These were laboratories in social experimentation in which the subjects could study themselves, and each other, in action. This meant that the only agenda or content was in the form of making something out of "nothing." In order to learn about oneself, and to learn about how groups work, people had to wallow in ambiguity and muddle through together.

This was a simple invention, producing a dilemma by having no agenda. In the process of making this void productive, people realized that *they* were the agenda. To study oneself in collaboration with others, publicly, is an anxious and awesome experience. Difficult but rewarding as this can be, the complexity and complications magnify many times when the laboratory is attempted in an organizational setting.[30] Personal revelations can become embarrassing and

29 Weschler, Irving; Massarik, Fred; Tannenbaum, Robert: The Self in Process: A Sensitivity Training Emphasis, Issues in Human Relations Training, NTL Washington, D.C. Selected Readings Series No. 5, 1962.

30 Atkins, Stuart and Kuriloff, Arthur H.: T-Group for a Work Team, op. cit.

even inappropriate in work groups.

As a result, another version of the laboratory method emerged. The emphasis was back to the content of the group's tasks, and the technical matters of group, and individual and group process observations were made only to facilitate the work of the group.

Becoming more sophisticated, these methods evolved into a movement called Organizational Development,[31] sponsored at first as a division of NTL. Much of the technology was geared to *entire organizations* as the client and OD practitioners worked throughout many departments simultaneously to effect major changes in all parts of the system. This was reminiscent of the early NTL hopes of effecting massive social change through the training of change agents based on the social emphasis of Kurt Lewin.

OD, as a massive change technology, did not prove practical, though many of its technologies—team building, conflict resolution, survey-feedback—are still widely practiced. But somewhere between the task focus of organizational development and the embarrassment of personal revelations in T-groups and Sensitivity Training, there was a need in the late sixties for structured, more manageable, less threatening, but personal ways of helping individuals and groups in a work setting.

In February of 1967, my efforts to fill that need began in the development of Life Orientations theory and its application through LIFO Training. Fifteen years have now passed, and I have distilled and crystallized the learning of those years in this book.

---

31 Burke, *Warner W. and Hornstein, Harvey A.:* The Social Technology of Organizational Development, *NTL Learning Resources Corp., Inc., Washington, D.C., 1972.*

15

ORGANIZATIONAL APPLICATIONS

LIFE ORIENTATIONS® TRAINING FOR INDIVIDUALS, PAIRS AND GROUPS

The Life Orientations model of human and organizational behavior has a wide variety of applications. It can be a self-contained program, or it can fit into existing programs. As a self-contained experience, it can start with individuals.

INDIVIDUAL APPLICATIONS

Individual counseling sessions with client and trainer can have as their focus boss-subordinate relationships, parent-child relationships, salesperson-customer relationships. It can also focus on intimate partners. The Life Orientations process for relationship improvement is identical in all relationships, irrespective of their nature.

This model was described in detail in the chapter entitled *The Case of the Apologetic Executive.* Discussions of differences with key people in one's life are central in leading to understanding, appreciating, utilizing, or organizing for the differences.

Self-appreciation and self-acceptance of one's strengths, excesses and blind spots are cornerstones for individual improvement. This goes hand in hand with trying to improve a key relationship. Self-understanding and developing a common language is a prerequisite for improving relationships. After the individual application with client and trainer, the other key person in the relationship can be brought into the process.

Often in pair applications, it is advisable first for the trainer and the separate individuals to meet to independently experience the training process. In this way, they become familiar with the language and the framework. This better prepares them to focus on each other, having first diffused any negative feelings. The individual session also reassures them of the positive aspects of Life Orientations Training and the objective discussion possible when they meet as a pair.

In the pair session, the focus is placed on each participant's uniqueness and preferences, and the expectations they have for each other that emerge from their orientations. Emphasis is on understanding what makes them different and what are some areas of similarity. This helps provide a common ground and shortens the distance between them. If differences are extreme, with no second or third orientations being similar, then the distance between them is larger, and the bridging strategy is more challenging.

Once they understand their differences, the next step is to *appreciate* the differences. This means that they each select strengths from the other that will be helpful to them, which can provide supplemental action, or at least a fresh perspective on problems and decisions. They contract to have the spirit of mutuality replace the irritation of misunderstanding differences.

A follow-up session or series of sessions can be set up to monitor progress and renegotiate their agreements. If it is too difficult over time to bridge their differences, then organizing for the differences is a final step. Organizing for differences means breaking down the areas of their work or family responsibilities into manageable segments. With these separate segments, each has the opportunity to do it completely his or her way without the aid of the other. When the segments are completely independent, they incorporate both parts into a unified plan of action.

Each can feel relieved that they have been "true" to their own way, but they will have lost the satisfactions that can come with mutuality. The plan or decision may also seem less unified or smooth, but it is a trade-off for employing strengths of two people who may be needed for their technical know-how, or two family members who are tied together by birth or the economies of living together.

WORKSHOP APPLICATIONS

This application centers on having a large number of people experience LIFO Training simultaneously. Up to twenty-five people can be managed successfully. Most often these participants do not work together, or they are not family members. However, workshops can be conducted with twosomes who are together, be their relationships parent-child, boss-subordinate, or intimate partners.

A minimum of one day is required in this application. In this day, all six strategies in the Training are covered—confirming, capitalizing, moderating, bridging, supplementing, and extending strengths. The emphasis is on personal productivity, stress control, restructuring the working or home environment consistent with strengths, and curbing excesses.

In the second day of a workshop, bridging is emphasized. Key relationships are re-examined to improve communications and increase satisfaction at home or at work.

With the large group, more time is spent on following the sequence and process structured into the Discovery and Communications workbooks. Less time is available for professional intervention and in-depth explanation of individual revelations or questions. Nevertheless, by forming pairs and threesomes from these "strangers," the facilitation role occurs between them. With a large group, the LIFO Training experience is more learner-centered, with the trainer acting in the capacity of a tour guide through the process, periodically presenting lecturettes on Life Orientations theory, and providing examples for clarification.

On several occasions, I have conducted workshops with as many as 350 participants. Though the trainer relates to an audience, not a group, many of the same insights can take place within the participants. But the size of the workshop makes it impersonal for the trainer, though not for the audience, because they are having guided, personal revelations which are immensely involving.

GROUP APPLICATIONS
OF THREE TO TWELVE PEOPLE

The same process involved in individual and pair counseling is also effective with small groups of three to twelve people. The group can be temporary, set up for a one-time project of a month to one year. Because time is of the essence, familiarity and communication must be accelerated.

Taking a temporary group through LIFO Training reveals how productivity can be encouraged, when it can be inhibited, or when and how the group can become counterproductive. Individual relationships are clarified as well as people's strengths, and potential excesses are highlighted. Group members learn which members can supplement them and how they can help each other with excesses. The group also can become aware of any missing perspective and which orientations they need in their planning and decision-making for total perspective. The application for a temporary group also applies to a permanent group which is just starting up.

An on-going group has additional needs because of its history. While the history has allowed time for work on relationships, a large residue of unresolved questions and tensions remain between the people. There has been disagreement and frustration centered around whose strengths will be used and recognized. Trust and mistrust has fluctuated, pairs have formed, and the favorites of the authority person have been identified. And Excellence, Action, Reason, and Harmony have been competing for first place as the group's standard. Added to this, the authority person becomes the example of which orientations and strengths get rewarded, ignored, or diminished.

These conditions lend themselves to team building. The LIFO Training process will objectively identify what is happening and will provide the direction for managing these pre-existing issues which have become the hidden agenda in the group.

The team building with LIFO Training places the group in disequilibrium by doing the unexpected. Instead of criticism and fault-finding, the process starts with positive regard for all the strengths in the group, irrespective of a person's rank or orientation. In a graphic way, the Training illustrates what has been going on in the group. It crystalizes the vague or incomplete understanding between people.

Having a common language and framework facilitates group members' talking with and about each other. The past history is focused forward in a non-threatening and action-directed way. This takes the sting or anger out of complaints about each other. It places people's expectations in a public framework that makes their fulfillment more possible. And energy, productivity, and satisfaction are not drained off in private puzzlement about each other, or in debilitating resentment or frustration.

VARIABLE ENTRY TEAM BUILDING

Entry involves a special dilemma. Most trainers agree that gaining entry to do team building is one of the most difficult tasks in Organizational Development. The problem with getting team building started involves a "vicious circle."

The dilemma is that where team building would be most helpful, is exactly where some team members will be most resistant to doing team building. The very norms, influence patterns, and self-images that need to be worked on in team building are the very things that create opposition to doing team building in the first place.

Here are three illustrations of the "vicious circle dilemma." First, self-serving attitudes can cause a managerial group to ignore complex problems that cut across functional lines. Team building would be the most effective way to awaken these managers to their corporate as well as departmental accountabilities. However, there is usually a big investment by some members of the team in maintaining the status quo. They can make their jobs easier by making sure to achieve their departmental goals at the expense of another department's, or even the overall unit's goals.

Secondly, defensiveness and competitiveness are frequently a way of organizational life. Low communication and even retaliation between managers can be the "prudent" course of action under "normal" conditions. Team building could free up the time, energy, and intelligence spent in these defensive efforts. Yet there is a vested interest in maintaining low communication. The risks of more open communication are often seen as too great. Open communication can reduce a manager's influence and increase his or her vulnerability with the boss and with peers.

The third situation where resistance is encountered involves the use of the collective talent in a managerial group.

Figure 1: VARIABLE ENTRY[sm] TECHNIQUES FOR TEAM BUILDING

ENTRY TECHNIQUE	BOSS-CENTERED[sm] TEAM BUILDING	MEMBER-CENTERED[sm] TEAM BUILDING	ONE-WAY[R] TEAM BUILDING	
EXTENT OF READINESS	The boss wants to clarify his or her expectations concerning how things should be done. Team members want clarify from the boss. Consultant works with boss and individual subordinates, or with boss and all team members in group setting.	The boss is not willing to participate in face-to-face team building, but wants team members to work out their differences. Team members are willing to work in pairs or in a group setting with the consultant.	One member of a team wants to improve relationships with team members or the boss, but they are not ready to participate in the improvement effort.	Boss and team members want to improve their work relationships, but are not willing to risk a face-to-face team building session.
ENTRY TOOLS	Discovery[R] Workbook with LIFO Survey (Boss only)	Communications Workbook with LIFO-AP Survey (All members) Discovery[R] Workbook with LIFO Survey	Discovery[R] Workbook with LIFO Survey (One member) Communications Workbook and LIFO-AP Survey	Discovery[R] Workbook with LIFO Survey (Boss and each member) Communications Workbook with LIFO-AP Survey

If this talent were applied to the problems of a manager's department, they could be solved quickly—benefiting the manager *and* the company as a whole. But reliance on team members never happens because some managers fear that using such methods would show them up and reflect a weakness that could ruin their careers. The give and take of team building could change this and multiply the group's effectiveness.

The old way and the only way to break these vicious circles was to work with the leader of the team and convince him or her that the group should be made to do team building. Even if members were anxious about it, overtly, or covertly resistant, or otherwise not favorably disposed, team building took place. In many cases, the trainer's choice was to do team building or nothing at all. This required the trainer to create a highly developed readiness for team building that was frequently unattainable.

There are three new ways to break the vicious circles. Trainers can have a new set of options that take advantage of the *different degrees of readiness* within a team. These new options are made possible by Variable Entry Techniques which allow the trainer to improve work relationships within a team whether only *one* team member is motivated to improve them, or the entire team is ready.

The variable entry techniques of LIFO Training include three new tools for gaining entry:

One-Way® Team Building	• Boss wants to clarify own expectations for team members.
Member-Centered℠ Team Building	• Boss unwilling to participate and members need to work on their relationships.
Boss-Centered℠ Team Building	• Some members are ready, or All want improvement but are unwilling to risk a face-to-face session.

Each of these techniques enables the trainer to take advantage of the readiness of team members while not forcing resistant members to participate beyond their readiness (see Figure 1.) Also, these techniques allow the trainer to start where the people want to start, while still having the necessary safeguards in place. For example, since the boss is not present in Member-Centered Team Building, this technique's design focuses exclusively on the relationships between and among the team members. It expressly makes focusing on the boss off limits. This is required to avoid activating any "depose the leader" dynamics that might otherwise occur.

All three techniques focus on managing differences and increasing positive influence. By going with the path of least resistance and greatest readiness, the trainer can begin the process of improvement with more teams than he or she could in the past. Each of the Variable Entry Techniques uses the Life Orientations theory and Training.

Working with the Life Orientations materials, the trainer helps his or her clients see that the key to influencing the other people is to *match their approach to the other person's orientation.* Team members sharpen their focus on influencing other people and improving their relationships by determining the other person's most preferred and least preferred orientations.

This tells them which approaches will have the most and least chance of having positive influence and reducing conflict over whose way is best. The trainer uses the training materials to make the team member aware of the other person's characteristic way of handling life and work problems. With this awareness, plus the knowledge of the approaches that he or she least prefers, the team member can intelligently plan how to work with each other more compatibly, without compromising their integrity.

When team members understand their differences in this objective context, rather than an emotionally charged, personal context, they are taking the first step required for effective team building. Using these core concepts and approaches of Life Orientations Training, each Variable Entry Technique is designed to help one or more team member manage differences and increase the constructive use of influence within the team. By impacting how differences are seen and utilized, and by increasing each member's influence, the trust level within the group can be raised sufficiently to allow additional improvement efforts to take place.

BOSS-CENTERED℠ TEAM BUILDING TO GAIN ENTRY

Boss-Centered Team Building focuses directly on the relationships between the boss and each member of the team. Much of the energy of subordinates is spent figuring out *how* to meet or deal with their boss's expectations. And the largest part of that energy is spent determining *the way* the boss wants things done. Often, without realizing it, people in organizations are constantly dealing with their boss's *preferences* concerning:

- how reports should be written
- the way the boss wants to get information in face-to-face discussions
- how the boss wants recommendations made to him or her
- the way subordinates should handle other people
- what kinds of issues should receive special attention

For example, in presentations some managers want only the bottom-line results without much elaboration on details. Other managers want a comprehensive, logically constructed presentation. Still others are more interested in knowing how key people feel about various aspects of the proposal. Each is operating out of a different orientation with a characteristically different pattern of preference. By learning which pattern of preferences goes with each of the four basic orientations to life, subordinates can reduce the time, energy, frustration and stress involved in the usual trial and error approach to determining the boss's expectations.

VERIFICATION STAGE

The first step is for the boss to clarify for himself or herself their own preference patterns. To accomplish this, the trainer has the boss complete a mini-training experience of one to two hours. This determines the boss's orientations and most preferred and least preferred ways of managing.

The boss reviews his or her preferred ways of making decisions, managing time, motivating subordinates, communicating with others, solving problems, negotiating agreements, planning, following up, and any other areas of special concern to the boss.

Next, the trainer has each subordinate identify areas where things are going well with the boss and areas where matters could be improved.

The trainer, the boss, and subordinates meet and the trainer explains the boss's preferences to the team members, then the areas where things are running smoothly and where additional work is required are discussed. After this, the team is ready to move to the next stage.

REINFORCEMENT STAGE

The boss limits his or her comments to positive reinforcements of where each subordinate has been meeting the boss's preferred ways of doing things. With the help of the trainer, the boss gives specific examples and instances where preferences are being met. The group compiles a list of those things that match the boss's preferred ways of being communicated with, influenced, and how he or she wants subordinates to perform on their job. Both the boss and the subordinates come away with a clear picture of what to keep doing.

CLARIFICATION STAGE

In the next stage the boss elaborates on his or her preferences in the areas that the team had marked for improvement. In each area the topic is freely discussed by the boss and team members. The boss describes the best way for subordinates to get through to him or her.

The trainer helps the boss and each subordinate review past critical incidents where there is a difference in orientation. The entire team begins to appreciate that in many situations there are not "right" and "wrong" ways of doing things; rather, there are simply more *preferred* ways.

The entire team frequently begins to appreciate their respective differences and becomes more tolerant of each other as a result. Often a more viable "live and let live" contract becomes possible.

With the trainer's assistance, subordinates take this information and develop a plan incorporating new approaches to the boss which are more consistent with the boss's orientation and detailed work preferences.

Each subordinate uses a Communications Guide and the information generated in the previous session to determine more compatible approaches to the boss. These new approaches are reviewed and discussed in a second clarification session where refinements are made with more information from the boss and the other team members.

NEGOTIATION STAGE

After the team has had sufficient time to implement their modified approaches, the trainer meets with the team to determine what areas require further modification. Some team members may experience difficulty in accommodating to the boss's preference. This can occur because of their own similarities or differences in preference. In the areas where people are experiencing difficulty, the trainer helps the subordinate and the boss decide on alternative approaches that are more livable and workable for both.

Boss-Centered Team Building helps subordinates learn how to utilize the boss as a resource for achievement, accomplishment, and career development. It helps the boss focus in the future on *what* goals need to be accomplished because there has been a resolution of *how* they need to be met. By cutting down on second guessing and the usual muddling through with trail and error, the entire team is able to systematically and consciously accomplish this important aspect of team development.

SUMMARY OF BOSS-CENTERED SM TEAM BUILDING

PURPOSE

Boss clarifies expectations concerning how he or she prefers the work to be accomplished. They explain and clarify for subordinates the most effective ways their subordinates can influence and communicate with them. This eliminates second guessing about how the boss wants things done. It answers the question for the boss, "How do my subordinates see me?" With the help of the trainer, the subordinates learn: (a) the best way to get through to the boss, and (b) how to get the boss to listen, accept and act on the team's ideas.

PROCEDURE

This is accomplished in a group or on a one-to-one basis

between supervisor and subordinate, with the guidance of the trainer, through the following steps:

1. *VERIFICATION*—"How I like things done." Boss identifies his or her orientations and preferences. Subordinates identify areas where things are going well with the boss and areas that need improvement. Boss and subordinates share their results.

2. *REINFORCEMENT*—"Keep doing what you are doing." Boss reinforces subordinates for approaches which meet his or her preferred ways. Boss gives specific examples of their preferences being met.

3. *CLARIFICATION*—"The best way to get through to me is . . . " Boss elaborates on their preferences and expectations for subordinates. Subordinates plan new approaches more consistent with Boss's orientation, using the boss's examples and a Communication Guide.

4. *NEGOTIATION*—"I'll do this if you'll do that." Some subordinates may encounter difficulty in accommodating to their boss's preferences because of their own similarities or differences in preference. Boss and subordinates decide on alternative approaches that are workable and livable for both.

MEMBER-CENTERED ᔆᴹ TEAM BUILDING TO GAIN ENTRY

Member-Centered Team Building focuses directly on the relationships between and among members of the team. This technique is designed to gain entry where the boss does not want to participate in team building with subordinates, but is willing to have his or her subordinates work together on their relationships with each other.

If the members of the team are willing to work with the trainer on improving their effectiveness with each other, the trainer can use this team building technique to help the team members clarify their expectations concerning their work preferences and clarify for each other the most effective ways they can influence and communicate with each other.

In the original contract with the boss and the subordinates, the trainer makes it clear that the members' relationships with the boss will not be on the agenda, since the boss will not be present.

The team members have the option of working on a one-to-one basis with the trainer being present, or collectively with the trainer in a group setting. A third option is to start the process on a one-to-one basis and then conclude it in a group meeting. This flexibility enables the trainer to capitalize on the extent of readiness of the people involved without creating unnecessary resistance at the outset.

This team building technique uses the Communications Workbook to identify how orientations work in a group. Each team member also uses the Discovery Workbook to describe their own work and life preferences.

VERIFICATION STAGE

In the first sessions, the trainer has the team members involved share their preferences and their strengths with each other. This can be done in a series of pairings or in a group. The members determine where they are in agreement concerning their perceptions of each other. Where there are differences, the trainer helps the team members compare their perceptions and the implications of their differences for their relationship.

The team members list those activities and transactions between them that are working well. Also they list areas where each member would like to see a change.

REINFORCEMENT STAGE

As a continuation of the first session, or as a follow-up session, the trainer has the team members tell each other where their preferences are being met. Each member explains their preferences in detail, giving specific examples of where they experienced each other in a compatible transaction. Pairs list the things they want to keep doing with regard to each other.

CLARIFICATION STAGE

Next, team members describe the best way to deal with each other on transactions or activities where problems may be occurring. Through an understanding of the other's preferences, they are able to pinpoint many of the causes of conflict between them. By using the Communication Guide, they learn which aspects to stress with each other when seeking cooperative effort. In many cases people have assumed that everyone has the same approach to problems as they do.

The trainer has each team member write out a new approach on troublesome projects or transactions. The new approach is designed to be more consistent with each of the other team members' orientations. Then the trainer and the team members involved exchange their plans for comment, modification, and agreement.

After the clarification session has been completed, the team members try out their new approaches with each other. After one to two months of experience, the trainer and team members meet to review how effectively their plans have worked.

NEGOTIATION STAGE

The trainer has each team member review their planned approaches with the other team members involved. Some members encounter difficulty in executing the new approaches. This may be due to too much similarity or difference in their respective preferences. Where difficulties have been experienced during the trial period, the trainer works with the team members on alternative approaches that are more workable between them.

After the boss has observed the relaxation in conflict as a result of the Member-Centered Team Building, the trainer can approach the boss to test his or her readiness for further improvement efforts. A possible next step for the boss is Boss-Centered Team Building.

SUMMARY OF MEMBER-CENTERED ^{SM} TEAM BUILDING

PURPOSE

Team members clarify their expectations concerning their preferences and clarify for co-workers the most effective ways they can influence and communicate with each other.

If the boss is unwilling to participate in team building, or is not prepared to do it, the team can still meet and work on improving its effectiveness. This technique answers the question, "What is the best way to get through to each other and listen, to accept and act on each other's ideas?"

PROCEDURE

This is accomplished in a group or on a one-to-one basis between team members, with the guidance of the trainer, through the following steps:

1. *VERIFICATION*—"How I like things to be done." Team members check out their orientations and preferences. They list situations where things are going well. They list areas that need improvement. Team members compare their results in a series of pairings or in a group.

2. *REINFORCEMENT*—"Keep doing what you are doing." Team members reinforce other team members who have predicted their preferred ways. They give specific examples of their preferences being met.

3. *CLARIFICATION*—"The best way to get through to me is . . . " Team members elaborate on their style preferences and expectations for other team members. Team members plan new approaches more consistent with each other's style using the specific examples of a Communication Guide.

4. *NEGOTIATION*—"I'll do this if you do that." Some team members may encounter difficulty in accommodating to other team members' preferences because of their own similarities or differences. Team members decide on alternative approaches that are workable and livable for each other.

THE ONE-WAY® TEAM BUILDING

Improving communications does not necessarily have to be accomplished in a mutual process. It can be done unilaterally, without the presence of the other person. We already have stored considerable information about each other. We need only retrieve it in an organized way.

For example, we have often heard others say:

"I'm the kind of person who . . . "
"That rubs me the wrong way."
"Now you're talking my language."
"That goes against my grain."
"That really fits."

People are telling us their preferences all the time. We

have data that has been registering with us from our first meetings. The difficulty is in retrieving it and making a coherent and usable picture out of this information.

The trainer uses the One-Way technique and materials to help the team members spot areas of differences with other members. Also, the trainer can use the materials to introduce the concepts and techniques of communications compatibility. This helps the team member determine alternative approaches that can be tried until improvement is reached with another person.

One of the Variable Entry Techniques designed to handle resistance caused by fear of emotional encounters is the One-Way Team Building Technique. This technique enables the trainer to work with one or more people who want to increase their effectiveness in the team by reducing unproductive competition, conflict, or defensiveness between themselves and one or more fellow team members—or even the boss.

This person, with the aid of the Communications Workbook, the LIFO-AP (Another Person) Survey, and the trainer's assistance, can *unilaterally* take steps to improve communications. The team member, together with the trainer, examines each relationship with fellow team members.

Taken one at a time, they are examined for ways to improve communication and influence. Tension and stress can be lowered by reducing conflict. The spiralling tendency for conflicts to escalate and deepen is stopped and reversed. Other team members can notice the change and frequently begin to respond to the person differently and more positively.

The trainer can help the team members break up any polarization from previous negative encounters. When a person does not understand another person, it is usually because he or she is expecting the other person to act as they do. When the other person acts differently, the client can feel threatened.

If the other person is not understandable or predictable, then the team members can become unsure of their ability to influence the other person. When this happens, the trust and openness towards the other person is proportionately reduced. Trust is experienced with those people we can influence.

Misunderstandings between team members usually lead to competitive stances. The thinking runs like this: He or she who is not like me may not be with me. He or she who is not with me is against me. Competition, in turn, leads to seeing the other person's actions as intending harm rather than intending support.

Suspicion can distort and selectively filter our constructive options. There is a tendency to define the conflicting interests between conflicting parties as unsolvable—except for a win-lose outcome. Though team members may not like unresolved conflict, they consider the alternatives to be even more threatening. Confrontation, they fear, can turn hurt feelings into hard feelings. Silent tensions can become shouting matches—reflecting badly on both parties.

The One-Way Team Building allows the trainer to move the team members to an objective basis for differences. With four orientations to life, with four fundamentally different ways of viewing the world, differences are in a new and constructive frame of reference. The team member discovers that it's OK and reasonable for the other team members to be different.

Then the trainer can point out to the team member that neither party in a relationship has to change their basic game plan or their personality in order to improve things between them. The team member needs to arrive at a negotiated solution to their differing interests.

Once the trainer has used One-Way Team Building to clear up the other person's intentions and orientations, the team member can revise his or her guesses about the other person, in light of the Life Orientations framework.

From this, the team members can formulate hypotheses about approaches that will be compatible with, and therefore acceptable to, the other person. This cuts down significantly on the usual trial and error process to figure out another person.

Once a single team member begins to act on his or her readiness to improve work relationships within the group, positive modeling occurs within the team. The competitive state within the team becomes less stable, allowing for additional efforts at increased cooperation.

Usually, differences of opinion are seen as a help by the other team members who interact with the team member who has experienced One-Way Team Building. The total amount of influence with group members increases. As a result, more trust is available between the team member and other members in the group.

A second application of the One-Way Team Building Technique centers on the *entire team.* When they want to improve their work effectiveness but are unwilling to risk a face-to-face team building session, the trainer can still captialize on their readiness. By working with each team member (including the boss) on an individual basis, each person can better understand each of the other team members and the boss. The boss studies each of his or her subordinates using the same approach. Working with the trainer, each person completes the One-Way Team Building process.

SUMMARY OF ONE-WAY®
TEAM BUILDING

PURPOSE

To build team work when the group is not prepared for a face-to-face process, or is not available geographically, or is just reluctant to participate.

When there is little or no support for team building from either the boss or team members, when there is low trust and high discomfort about meeting together, team improvement is *still possible.* The boss and team members work privately with the trainer, using the special One-Way technique to improve relationships within the team.

In this application, team members and/or boss, *unilaterally* focus and clarify their thinking about other people in their groups in the non-judgmental Life Orientations language and materials. This helps them with blind spots and untested assumptions about their group relationships. It helps them see other team members in a more individualized and positive way. In One-Way Team Building, *significant clarification* develops because people take responsibility themselves for improving their group relationships.

PROCEDURE

1. Team members and/or boss identify their own orientations and their meaning for relationships. Then they identify each other's orientations with the Life Orientations AP Survey in the Communications Workbook.
2. Individually, team members consider the AP Survey implications of each other's preferences, looking for similarities or differences.
3. Team members check the Communications Guide to see if their approaches are consistent with the other team members' values and preferences.
4. They modify and match their approaches to other team members' values and preferences in a way most comfortable with their own.

The three Variable Entry Techniques for doing team building provide a wide range of starting points for the trainer. They are designed to get development of a team started without creating additional resistance.

Each technique uses a variation of the Life Orientations model and a positive, no-fault, judgment-free approach. The entry point is used to increase one or more team member's ability to manage differences by using compatible approaches to their own and the preferences of other team members.

The Boss-Centered Team Building will have an appeal to many team leaders who are comfortable in their role of authority, but would feel threatened by the unstructured give and take of more traditional forms of team building.

The Member-Centered Technique makes it possible for the trainer to work with team members to improve team work or reduce conflict, even if the leader of the team is not available.

The One-Way Technique allows the trainer to start efforts that can achieve similar results to traditional team building, even if some members are unwilling to participate, or where a group setting is too threatening.

Each technique can be used separately, or as a progression, depending on the potential and limits in the situation facing the trainer.

The above applications of Life Orientations Theory and Training are self-contained. They stand alone. However, the Training can fit into existing courses and programs—from one-day programs to five-day programs. Often the Life Orientations segment is used as a beginning to break the ice. It frees people to talk about themselves and organizational problems. It produces a more supportive, problem-solving climate.

Here is a sample of the variety of traditional training topics that are personalized for the trainee by the Life Orientations framework. In addition, the personal focus helps the trainee internalize the learning of the more abstract training topics.

LIFE ORIENTATIONS TRAINING APPLICATIONS

LEADERSHIP

1. Demonstrates that there is no one best way to be a successful leader or manager.
2. Shows people how to capitalize on their unique leadership style and how to motivate others through their unique style.

MANAGEMENT BY OBJECTIVES

1. Ties in group objectives with the personal objectives and orientations of people.
2. Encourages and builds commitment to objectives by structuring them to meet the preferred styles and values of those responsible for achieving them.

DELEGATION

1. Permits assignment of tasks and projects to be executed in a way most consistent with people's unique orientation and strengths.
2. Emphasizes compatibility of orientations and strengths with task or project being assigned.

PROBLEM SOLVING

1. Allows people to use their own unique strengths and style to find solutions to problems that they can live with.
2. Builds appreciation of the different but equally effective approaches to solving a problem.
3. Helps people see the four sides to every problem to gain a more complete and enduring solution.

MOTIVATION

1. Shows how to get others into action through the personal motives of each orientation.
2. Identifies best way to structure a job to capitalize on the strengths and satisfactions of others.

COACHING AND COUNSELING

1. Whether one is the coach or counselee, it helps people by using an approach that is acceptable to their preferred style.
2. Focuses on strengths rather than weaknesses.
3. Provides relevant options in selecting growth and development targets.

STRESS MANAGEMENT

1. Identifies the personal and situational causes of stress.
2. Reduces counter-productive, excessive use of strengths by correcting the underlying personal and situational causes of stress.
3. Provides techniques for communicating with people in stress and for helping them out of stress.

CONFLICT RESOLUTION

1. Focuses on style differences as a major contributing factor to conflict.
2. Resolves differences by fostering understanding and appreciation of all orientations.
3. Provides win-win strategies for negotiating differences and achieving cooperation.

TEAM BUILDING

1. Combines strengths to achieve mutual satisfaction and maximum productivity.
2. Recognizes and encourages the unique contributions of people with different strengths.
3. Facilitates team building even if all members do not wish to participate—with One-Way, Member-Centered, or Boss-Centered team building.

Whether used within an existing program, or within a self-contained program, Life Orientations theory and Training has a significant impact on individuals, pairs, and groups.

In the next chapter, I have reproduced the comments and evaluations about the Training by a diverse group of professionals. They represent a wide spectrum of organizations. And I have also included my summary conclusions about Life Orientations theory and Training, and why it has such appeal and impact.

16

AFTERTHOUGHTS

HOW I PLAYED THE GAME

It is now fifteen years since the first development of Life Orientations Training. Those earlier years seem primitive and skeletal compared with the advanced developments which have appeared in this book. At first, there was only the Life Orientations survey and a three-page description of the four orientations, their strengths, and the theory behind them. Then the six strategies emerged as an organizing principle and an application focus.

From that beginning, Life Orientations Training has not only expanded in content, but in worldwide utilization. Half the Fortune 500 companies are using it, as well as over 100 universities, and many hospitals, churches, government agencies, and professionals in private practice. Over 5,000 organizations and one million people have experienced LIFO Training.

In 1968, the program had its introduction in a small group of organizations such as the American Cancer Society, U.S. Steel, Mattel Toys, State of California, and in my class in Human Factors in Management at UCLA. By 1972, many organizational trainers wanted to learn to teach the program and, at that point, the professional licensing program began. Many of these professionals and their organizations still conduct the Training. It has stood the test of time and the rigorous evaluation of professionals and their client organizations.

Those who conduct Life Orientations Training can speak more objectively about it. Their comments and commendations are condensed statements about its usefulness and effectiveness. As you will notice, trainers like using the short form "LIFO Training" as the program's title.

Here are some typical statements from professionals who represent a wide variety of disciplines and a diverse group of people.

"Each organization and each couple has found important insights more visible through LIFO Training. I use it with regularity in team building, with school system personnel, in stress management workshops, in marital therapy and pre-marital counseling and in dozens of other settings. It is the most helpful entry vehicle I have found for almost any O.D. intervention."

> Larry Webb, Ph. D.
> Consultant-Therapist
> Human Systems Development Association

"Have used LIFO Training extensively in Police Management Field. Police managers are amazed at the differences in people and the effect these differences have on productivity—and how essential it is in today's economy."

> Norman Pomrenke
> Director, Southern Police Institute
> University of Louisville

"When a person says, 'Yes, that's me. Now I know what to do to improve myself,' it's giving that person the skills and techniques to move beyond self-defeating behavior by recognizing one's style, and the triggers to excess. Knowing that 'my own style is OK', begins that process."

> Larry Ferguson, Ph. D.
> Clinical Director
> Link Care Center

"I find it most useful in the help it is giving in marriage counseling."

> Rev. D. C. Kalweit, Senior Pastor
> Messiah Lutheran Church

"One of the best tools for feedback process in team-building—easy identification by managers to styles—non-threatening, easily understood and very well liked by management groups."

Stan Abrahamson,
Director, Engineering Services
Control Data Corporation

"Its non-threatening approach in getting interpersonal issues out in the open, and an 'it's OK to be me' mode, while emphasizing accommodation."

John Miller
Administrator, Management Development
Blue Cross of Southern California

"One of my colleagues had a strong opposition to almost anything related to Organizational Development. He has accepted the LIFO program, is extending it to his people, and is adjusting his style very beneficially."

F. D. Lorey, Director, Melting Technology
Corning Glass Works

"I feel that it is a powerful model of Human Behavior."

Herman Englander
Consultant

"See people's indifference or fear turn to curiosity, then interest, then fascination . . . I have worked a lot with educators who tend to be either indifferent or fearful toward instruments. LIFO Training helps introduce them to information that is growth producing—often they have not had this experience before . . ."

Oron South, Ph. D.
Florida State University

"I believe strongly in LIFO Training as a way to get a handle on managing differences. It is simple and effective. It is compatible with every other training I've been involved with before and after my certification."

Dallas Porter
District Training Coordinator
Arizona Department of Economic Security

"LIFO Training has proven, via a variety of applications, to be the single most useful H.R.D. tool I have encountered. Am currently using it very successfully in team building interventions and in a Personal Growth workshop."

> Stephen F. Royka
> Manager, Employee Development
> Xerox Corporation

"Easy to understand, good way to elicit feedback and dialogue."

> Joanna Weichert, Personnel Manager
> General Foods, Cranbury Center

"The LIFO Training materials are not shallow—my own depth of awareness increases with every use, formally and informally. Therefore the effectiveness for me and others is enlarged."

> Judy Baker
> Manager, Human Resources Development
> Cray Research

"I continue to be delighted at the way LIFO Training opens up channels of communications in groups. A common vocabulary quickly develops and the level of sharing (read risking) deepens."

> Rev. Jan C. Walker
> Lutheran Church

"I was so strong in Conserving-Holding and Supporting-Giving that I often was not aware of the needs of those I was trying to 'train'. Through plans and feedback, I increased my Adapting-Dealing and got much better results, was more relaxed, and can use myself as one example of how LIFO Training does work!"

> John Burpee
> Director, Employee Relations
> Saxon Industries, QPP Division

"One of the most excellent means of facilitating feedback among a staff team that I know—focuses on solvable problems and 'personality issues'."

> Rev. John Bryan
> Presbyterian Church

"People can relate to the feedback generated and directly apply it to their life or job. I've been using it successfully for nine years."

> Bruce Bolen,
> Manager, Personnel & Administration
> Canon Business Machines

"Using LIFO Training with first-line supervisors is such an eye-opener for them—to learn that they have a style and can use it. Capitalizing on their strengths and those of others while recognizing and curbing their excesses is exciting for them."

> Charles Gompertz, President
> The Gompertz Management Group

"Gives people entry and language to talk about themselves in ways they couldn't before."

> R. R. Ott, Senior Training Associate
> U.S. Steel Corporation

"I used LIFO Training with career course students while assigned to the U.S. Army Chaplain School. LIFO Training was included as part of our curriculum required for each student. It was not unusual to have a student refer to it as one of the highlights of the 21-week course."

> Marion Pember, Chaplain (LTC)
> U.S. Army

"The best 'human resource' tool I've found. The most 'necessary' prelude to any O.D., M.B.O., or team development effort. Planning is empty without it. In use with the university's management efforts, the 'cognitive' immediacy is staggering to longtime trainers."

> Paul Savko, Director, University Center
> University of Texas

"As a psychologist I find LIFO Training so helpful in getting people away from the sick model—'it's my sickness's fault,' to a more productive way of looking at themselves."

> Kenneth Visser, Ph. D., Branch Manager
> De Soto Mental Health Clinic

"The usefulness and applicability of using LIFO Training in churches is what I like. I have done one short workshop in a church and will be doing more. They loved it!"

> Jonathon Hess
> Vice President, Student Affairs
> Westmont College

"It's potent material."

> Bill Snider
> Director, Management Development
> Transamerica Financial Corporation

"In a leadership styles week-long workshop with small groups, I used LIFO Training in the third day to give the small group a backdrop to look at behaviors they had displayed during the week. The insights were very powerful and long lived. They took the workbook to work through with the same small group (eight people). It was the benchmark."

> Al Hanner, President
> Leadership Training, Incorporated

It is difficult for me to experience the meaning of the widespread impact of Life Orientation theory and Training. Intellectually I can understand it, but only by what the trainers have said in their positive evaluations. Emotionally, it has happened "out there" with clients unknown to me. My direct experience with my own clients is the only source of my full realization of the meaning of the Training to other people.

From my own experience, and that of other people, I have come to some conclusions about the ever-expanding appeal of the Training, and where it will be ten years from now.

The appeal and the usefulness of the Training can be summarized by six key points:

FOCUS ON STRENGTHS. People can concentrate on developing their strengths, rather than dwelling on weaknesses or shortcomings.

NON-THREATENING. It is a structured, directed process that places control for self-revelation and self-disclosure in the hands of the learner.

EVERYDAY LANGUAGE. Ideas are expressed in everyday language, not negative jargon or psychological terms which require a special background.

PROVIDES OPTIONS. Selecting one or several LIFO Strategies for development allows freedom of choice rather than forced learning.

NO IDEAL MODEL. Emphasis is placed on making the most of one's unique personality, rather than attempting to follow an ideal model of a person or occupational role.

SELF-NORMATIVE. Relief from judgmental comparisons is possible because there are no norms or standards about what is best, what is good or bad, right or wrong—only what is best and right for the person in relationship to others.

Looking ahead, what is in store for Life Orientations Training? Over the next ten years, the thrust will be on expanding the newly formed Career and Life ManagementSM Institute. Under the Institute, two major functions will be served, teaching and research.

The teaching will follow the Life Orientations Training curriculum which will consist of a basic two-day workshop, with the follow-up possibilities of a series of one-day workshops. These will be about Personal Productivity, Stress Control, Capitalizing on Strengths, and on Key Relationships, with separate workshops for parent-child, boss-employee, teacher-student, salesperson-customer relationships, as well as intimate partner relationships.

A second curriculum will center on managing Career Advancement. This will also start with a two-day workshop. A modified version of LIFO Training will be a major component of the workshop. A series of one-day follow-up workshops will be available, focusing on Pre-Retirement, Mid-Career, Renewal, and Early Career Advancement Strategies.

The third curriculum will emphasize Job Performance and Productivity for both individuals and organizations. This begins with a two-day workshop, incorporating Life Orientations Training concepts and materials. Follow-up one-day workshops will deal with Performance Appraisal, Team Building, and Productivity.

Besides teaching, the Career and Life Management Institute will have a research function. One major area of study will be the development of orientations in the early years and the family influence on choice of orientations. Another major area will be on the effect of combinations of orientations between student and teacher on learning and achievement. The third major research area will be on the topic of compatibility in key relationships. Combinations of orientations will be studied to better understand their mutual impact and discover what relationship strategies and tactics will advance the relationship.

Well, that is my dream for the next ten years. It is a possible dream. It is possible because the preceding fifteen years have laid the groundwork in establishing and developing Life Orientations Theory and Training. Completing this book has consolidated what I have learned and what I believe. I hope it makes a difference in your life.

BIBLIOGRAPHY

Adler, Alfred. *The Science of Living.* Doubleday & Co., Inc., New York, 1969.

Appley, Mortimer and Trumbull, Richard. *Psychological Stress.* Appleton-Century-Croft, New York, 1967.

Atkins, Stuart and Kuriloff, Arthur H. *T Group for a Work Team.* Journal of Applied Behavioral Science, Vol. 2, No. 1, Jan.-Mar., 1966.

Atkins, Stuart. *A Moment in Forever.* Journal of Applied Behavioral Science, Vol. 3, No. 4, 1967.

Atkins, Stuart. (An Interview with) *Helping People Deal With Their Differences—An O.D. Direction.* Journal of Applied Behavioral Science, Vol. 13, No. 1, 1977.

Bach, George. *Intimate Enemy.* George Widen, New York, 1970.

Berne, Eric. *Games People Play.* Ballantine Books, New York, 1964.

Blake, Robert and Mouton, Jane. *The Managerial Grid.* Gulf Publishing Co., Houston, 1964.

Bradford, Leland P.; Gibb, Jack R.; Berne, Kenneth D. *T-Group Theory and Laboratory Methods.* John Wiley & Sons, Inc., New York, 1964.

Bromley, D. B. *Personality Descriptions in Ordinary Language.* John Wiley & Sons, Inc., New York, 1977.

Burke, Warner W. and Hornstein, Harvey A. *The Social Technology of Organizational Development.* NTL Learning Resources Group, Inc. Fairfax, Virginia, 1972.

Buss, Allan and Poley, Wayne. *Individual Differences: Traits and Factors.* Gardner Press, Inc., New York, 1976.

Carson, Robert. *Interaction Concepts of Personality.* Aldine Publishing Co., Chicago, 1969.

Datan, N. and Ginsberg, L. H. *Life Span Developmental Psychology.* Academic Press, New York, 1975.

Edwards, Allen L. *The Measurement of Personality Traits by Scales and Inventories.* Holt, Rinehart & Winston, New York, 1970.

Erikson, E. H. *Childhood and Society.* W. W. Norton & Co., Inc., New York, 1963.

Erikson, E. H. *Adulthood.* W. W. Norton, New York, 1978.

Fadiman, James and Frager, Robert. *Personality and Personal Growth.* Harper & Row, New York, 1976.

Friedman, Meyer and Rosenman, Ray. *Type A Behavior and Your Heart.* Alfred Knopf, New York, 1974.

Fromm, Erich. *Man For Himself.* Holt, Rinehart & Winston, Inc., New York, 1947.

Fromme, Allan. *The Ability to Love.* Wilshire Book Co., North Hollywood, California, 1965.

Goldstein, Kenneth, M. and Blackman, Sheldon. *Cognitive Style.* John Wiley & Sons, Inc., New York, 1978.

Greenwald, Jerry. *Be the Person You Were Meant to Be.* Simon & Schuster, New York, 1973.

James, Muriel and Jongeward, Dorothy. *Born to Win.* Addison-Wesley, Reading, Mass., 1971.

James, Muriel, and Trata, John. *The OK Boss.* Addison-Wesley, Inc., Reading, Mass., 1975.

Jung, Carl. *Modern Man in Search of a Soul.* Harcourt Brace Jovanovich, New York, 1933.

Jung, Carl; Campbell, Joseph—Ed. *The Portable Jung.* Viking Press, New York, 1971.

Kelly, George A. *A Theory of Personality—The Psychology of Personal Constructs.* W. W. Norton & Co., Inc., New York, 1963.

Koch, Sigmund—Ed. *Psychology: A Study of a Science, Vol. 2, General Systematic Formulations, Learning, and Special Processes.* McGraw-Hill, New York, 1959.

Koch, Sigmund—Ed., *Psychology: A Study of a Science, Vol. 3, Formulations of the Person and the Social Context,* McGraw-Hill, New York, 1959.

Laing, P. D.; Phillipson, H.; Lee, A. R. *Interpersonal Perception.* Harper & Row, New York, 1966.

Luft, Joseph. *Of Human Interaction.* National Press, Palo Alto, 1969.

Luft, Joseph. *Group Process.* Mayfield Publishing Co., Palo Alto, 1970.

Mahler, M. D. *On Human Symbiosis and The Vicissitudes of Individuation.* I. U. P., New York, 1969.

Maslow, Abraham. *The Far Reaches of Human Nature,* Viking Press, New York, 1971.

Maslow, Abraham. *Toward a Psychology of Being.* D. Van Nostrand Co., Inc., Princeton, 1962.

Pfeiffer, William; Heslin, Richard; Jones, John. *Instrumentation in Human Relations Training.* University Associates, Inc., San Diego, 1976.

Progoff, Ira. *At a Journal Workshop.* Dialogue House Library, New York, 1975.

Rogers, Carl. *Client-Centered Therapy.* Houghton Mifflin Co., Boston, 1951.

Rogers, Carl. *On Becoming a Person.* Houghton Mifflin Co., Boston, 1970.

Sager, C. J. *Marriage Contracts and Couple Therapy.* Bruner/Mazel, New York, 1976.

Schiffman, Muriel. *Gestalt Self Therapy.* Self Therapy Press, Menlo Park, 1971.

Selye, Hans. *The Stress of Life.* McGraw-Hill Book Co., New York, 1978.

Shapiro, David. *Neurotic Styles.* Basic Books, New York, 1965.

Spielberger, Charles D.; Sarason, Irwin G. *Stress and Anxiety,* Vol. 5. John Wiley & Sons, New York, 1978.

Watzlawick, P.; Bevin, J. H.; Jackson, D. G. *Pragmatics of Human Communications.* W. W. Norton, New York, 1967.

Wilson, Colin. *New Pathways in Psychology, Maslow and The Post Freudian Revolution.* New American Library, Inc., New York, 1972.